# The Fuel Project Guide To:

# REVELATION

by Mark Fairley

# CONTENTS

# INTRODUCTION

Many words have been used to describe the book of Revelation. "Strange", "Awe-inspiring", "Confusing", "Amazing", "Intimidating", "Unique", "Terrible", "Majestic" and "Mysterious" might be just a few.

It divides opinion like no other too. Throughout history it has been derided on the one hand as a book with 'as many riddles as there are words', a 'farrago of baseless fantasies' and 'a haphazard accumulation of weird symbols'. The Reformer, Martin Luther, had such a low view of the book that he said 'it is a pity it ever got into the New Testament.' His fellow Reformers held a similar position.

On the other hand, just as many have had a much higher view. It has been called 'the only masterpiece of pure art in the New Testament' and 'beautiful beyond description' by others. 'A book full of blessings and riches' was the opinion of William Barclay.

God's opinion of it is perhaps the highest of them all. It is the only book in the Bible that contains an explicit blessing for those who read it:

*"God blesses the one who reads the words of this prophecy to the church, and he blesses all who listen to its message and obey what it says, for the time is near." (Revelation 1:3)*

It is the only book that contains a curse for those who dare to tamper with it too:

*"And I solemnly declare to everyone who hears the words of prophecy written in this book: If anyone adds anything to what*

*is written here, God will add to that person the plagues described in this book. And if anyone removes any of the words from this book of prophecy, God will remove that person's share in the tree of life and in the holy city that are described in this book." (Rev 22:18-19)*

With these warnings in mind, it's with a great degree of reverence, respect and care that I approach this special book.

One thing we should not be, however, is intimidated. God gave us Revelation because he wants us to read it and understand. As the title of the book suggests, it is designed to reveal; not hide. It takes a certain degree of time, patience and Biblical literacy to decode the imagery within but in doing so, we discover that it's exactly the vividness of the imagery that gives it such depth and richness of insight. It will reward all who take the time to immerse themselves in it. That was certainly my experience as I undertook this study. And it's for this reason that I recommend you really take your time with this book and go through it slowly. When there are footnotes or references provided, I recommend that you look them up straight away. Read Appendix items before proceeding with the main body of text too. And where Bible verses have been cited, take the time to find them. Indeed, you'll find it useful to keep your Bible open beside you as you go. Take a deep soak in the message.

The Fuel Guide to Revelation has been written with certain guiding principles in mind.

The first, and most important principle, is to use the KIS approach - Keep It Simple! If Revelation appears to be saying something then that's probably what it says. Too often people come to this book with a pre-conceived theology formed from extra-Biblical sources and then try to mould the imagery to fit what they already want to believe. We call that eisegesis. It just means imposing a meaning onto a text that comes from the interpreter's own ideas or bias. That's not what we want. Indeed, those who go down that road will end up tying themselves up in all kinds of knots. What we want is exegesis. Exegesis means pulling out of the text the plain intended meaning within its original context. Keep it simple. No matter how uncomfortable the truth seems to be.

Part of the KIS approach also means understanding that Revelation is written chronologically. The recurrence of the phrase, "and then I saw..." or "and then I heard..." tells us that John - the writer - is having the future revealed to him in a sequence. There is no reason why God would deliberately confuse John, or us, by presenting information to him in a chronological sequence which is completely irrelevant to how the end-times will actually play out. We mustn't fall into the trap of coming to Revelation with a "Pick 'n' Mix" approach. We cannot skew the timeline to suit our own ends. We are not at liberty to pluck out verses here and there or to move chapters around to fit with our preconceived notions. Once we understand this, many of today's popular ideas about Revelation and the end-times are quickly demolished.

With all this in mind, my hope is that the Bible itself will do the talking. I have copied the entire book of Revelation in the pages that follow and then merely inserted commentary and supporting passages from other parts of the Bible wherever it is helpful for deeper insight. All text from Revelation is written in red to help with identification and to let the reader know when we are moving forward in the book. If you are reading on a device that does not support colour text, I hope this will not impair your enjoyment.

Most of all, I hope you will find this guide useful in understanding how the future of the world will come to pass and that it will help to focus our minds as we hurtle towards Jesus' second coming.


Mark Fairley

The Fuel Project

# CHAPTER 1. WE HAVE TRIBULATION

*"In the world you will have tribulation. But take heart; I have overcome the world." (John 6:33)*

Christians are now the most persecuted people group on the entire planet. The International Society for Human Rights, a secular observatory based in Frankfurt, Germany, says 80% of all acts of religious discrimination in the world today are directed at Christians.[1] Italian sociologist and author, Dr Massimo Introvigne recently stated that a Christian dies every 5 minutes in the world today because of their faith.[2] In a 2012 report for Civitas, researcher and author, Rupert Shortt, agreed stating, *"It is generally accepted that many faith-based groups face discrimination or persecution to some degree. A far less widely grasped fact is that Christians are targeted more than any other body of believers."*[3] Dr Carl Moeller of Open Doors USA, citing independent research from the Pew Forum on Religion & Public Life said, *"Whether you count martyrs, those killed, or you count those living [under oppressive] regimes, sizable Christian populations live under extreme restrictions in places like China, Indonesia, and of course the Middle East."*[4] Even secular politicians such as German chancellor Angela Merkel, have recently broken boundaries of political correctness to state on record that Christianity is now the most persecuted religion in the world.[5] Ex-French President, Nicolas Sarkozy, during his time in office called it "ethnic cleansing."[6]

You won't hear much about the growing tide of violence, harassment, rape, destruction of property and murder of Christians from the Western media. In fact, journalists like The

Atlantic's Jeffrey Goldberg, are calling this *"one of the most undercovered stories in international news."*[7] However, the truth is very simply that nothing puts a person at more risk in the world today than simply daring to identify themselves as a follower of Jesus Christ. There is a deep and deepening hatred of Christianity. To turn the language of secular society back on itself, the world is becoming increasingly Christophobic. You might say, becoming increasingly anti-Christ.

Hatred for Christ, his message and his followers, may be growing in the world today but it's nothing new. Jesus of Nazareth was stripped, scourged, spat upon, mocked, nailed to a cross of wood and hung up to die naked in front of a baying mob. Each of his disciples would go on to live a persecuted life of their own and all but one would die a martyrs death. Jesus told them ahead of time that this would happen saying:

*"And everyone will hate you because you are my followers..."* *(Mark 13:13)*

He also told them:

*"If the world hates you, remember that it hated me first. The world would love you as one of its own if you belonged to it, but you are no longer part of the world. I chose you to come out of the world, so it hates you. Do you remember what I told you? 'A slave is not greater than the master.' Since they persecuted me, naturally they will persecute you. And if they had listened to me, they would listen to you."* *(John 15:18-20)*

Later Jesus would pray for his disciples saying:

*"...the world hates them because they do not belong to the world, just as I do not belong to the world."* *(John 17:14)*

Peter was one who understood the clarity of his Master's message. Later, he would write to the church in Asia Minor as it began to suffer persecution telling them: *"So then, since Christ suffered physical pain, you must arm yourselves with the same attitude and be ready to suffer too...don't be surprised at the fiery trials you are going through, as if something strange were happening to you." (1 Peter 4:1, 12)*

Peter here is telling the church that tribulation is absolutely normal and a natural consequence of following Jesus in a world that despises him. Clearly if Peter felt the need to write this letter, the church in Asia Minor probably *was* surprised that it was having to suffer for the name of Christ! Peter wrote this to reassure them that there was really nothing to be surprised about. Those who would follow Jesus would have to be prepared to suffer as he suffered.

The apostle Paul wrote to his young protégé Timothy, to warn him of this fact too. He wrote, *"Yes, and everyone who wants to live a godly life in Christ Jesus will suffer persecution." (2 Timothy 3:12)* The subtext of Paul's message is that the more godly you are, the worse things will become!

Paul gave a similar message to the churches in Lystra, Iconium and Antioch saying that, *"we must suffer many hardships to enter the Kingdom of God." (Acts 14:22)* We *must* suffer. Not, *"we may suffer."* Suffering is laid down as a pre-requisite.

If there's one thing that the early church was warned to prepare itself for... if there was one thing that it could be absolutely certain of... it's that they would suffer much tribulation. Persecution was an inescapable, natural and even necessary consequence of following Jesus Christ in a world that hates him. And if the warnings weren't explicit enough, Jesus even went so far as to say that many would be called to give up their lives here for him.

*"Then Jesus said to his disciples, "If any of you wants to be my follower, you must turn from your selfish ways, take up your cross, and follow me. If you try to hang on to your life, you will lose it. But if you give up your life for my sake, you will save it. (Matt 16:24-25)*

For 2,000 years these words of warning have proven to be well founded.

## TRIBULATION THROUGH THE AGES

It started with the stoning of Stephen, the first martyr. Simply for preaching the gospel, Stephen was dragged outside the city walls of Jerusalem and pelted to death *(Acts 7)*. The book of Hebrews describes the suffering of those that followed in the ensuing years:

*"But others were tortured, refusing to turn from God in order to be set free. They placed their hope in a better life after the resurrection. Some were jeered at, and their backs were cut open with whips. Others were chained in prisons. Some died by stoning, some were sawed in half, and others were killed with the sword. Some went about wearing skins of sheep and goats, destitute and oppressed and mistreated. They were too good for this world, wandering over deserts and mountains, hiding in caves and holes in the ground." (Hebrews 11:35-38)*

This description of Christian suffering was written around 68AD - just a few years after Emperor Nero had taken to the throne of the Roman Empire (64AD). Nero's hatred for Christians has become infamous but the persecution that he inflicted on them actually started in relatively minor ways. It began with confiscation of property and vandalization of homes. Occasionally there were prison sentences. Gradually, the antipathy grew and his violence towards them became ever more savage. The horrific coliseum shows were established where Christians were put to death in front of a baying stadium for sport. They were sewn up inside the skins of wild animals and then set upon by dogs who would shred them to death. They were tied to poles in arenas of lions. Nero seemed to take great pleasure in inventing new ways of ending Christian lives. Perhaps one of the most gruesome methods was by tying them to poles in his garden, covering them in wax or oil and then setting alight to become living human torches to illuminate the night.

When a fire ravaged the city of Rome, burning for six days and seven nights and causing three quarters of the city to end up in ruins, the citizens of Rome were furious with Nero. They believed he had not done enough to control the disaster and there were even rumours that this megalomaniac had started the fire himself so that he might rebuild it according to his own image. In order to deflect the anger of the people, he made scapegoats of the already despised Christians. The Roman historian Tacitus describes it like this:

*"Therefore, to stop the rumour [that he had set Rome on fire], he [Emperor Nero] falsely charged with guilt, and punished with the most fearful tortures, the persons commonly called Christians, who were [generally] hated for their enormities. Christus, the founder of that name, was put to death as a criminal by Pontius Pilate, procurator of Judea, in the reign of Tiberius, but the pernicious superstition - repressed for a time, broke out yet again, not only through Judea, - where the*

*mischief originated, but through the city of Rome also, whither all things horrible and disgraceful flow from all quarters, as to a common receptacle, and where they are encouraged. Accordingly first those who were arrested who confessed they were Christians; next on their information, a vast multitude were convicted, not so much on the charge of burning the city, as of "hating the human race."*

The actions of Nero set a precedent and the persecution of Christians continued in Rome under succeeding Emperors. Domitian, Trajan, Marcus Aurelius, Septimus Severus, Decius, Valerian, Maximus the Thracian, Aurelian, Diocletian, Galerius and Julian all oversaw waves of terrible tribulation for the church throughout the Roman Empire.

If the aim was to extinguish Christianity by this method, it did not have the required effect. If anything, persecution seemed to make the church stronger. It grew and kept growing, no matter how harshly the believers were treated. Indeed, when the growing presence of Christianity seemed to be threatening the very stability of Rome itself, it became clear that a different approach was required to subdue the Christian movement. Instead of attacking the church from without by way of violence, Emperor Constantine decided to legalise it and parasitically take it over from within. Like the Costa Rican wasp parasite that is able to live within the bodies of a host spider, hijacking their brain functions and causing them to act as they desire, Constantine was able to merge the Roman church with the Roman political system and to subsequently control it for his own purposes. Over time, the superstitions, polytheism and politics of Rome were woven into the church there and by doing so, it became a pagan, institutionalised, hollow parody of

Biblical faith. It became Catholicism. Roman paganism in a Christian shell.

In Europe, this Catholic church reigned throughout a thousand-year period of ignorance known as The Dark Ages. During this time, the Bible was taken away from the common man and its text was deliberately shrouded behind the Latin language - a dead tongue than none could read or speak except the Clergy. This created a dependency on the Clergy who abused their power, threatening damnation and hell to anyone who rejected their corrupt authority. Those who dared to own or read the Bible for themselves, or to foster a personal relationship with Christ outwith the institution, were dealt with harshly. Pope Innocent III summed up their attitude saying, *"Anyone who attempts to construe a personal view of God which conflicts with Church dogma must be burned without pity."* Indeed, anyone who rejected their unbiblical dogma was denounced as a heretic, hunted down, imprisoned, tortured and often killed. Many such 'heretical' groups came and went throughout these years, most notably the Waldensians. In other words, a great many of the people on the receiving end of the Catholic Inquisitions were actually Christians! Sincere men and women trying to practice a Biblical faith as best they knew how with the limited information they had available to them at a dark time.

During the Reformation, with the invention of the printing press and an increase in literacy levels, Bible translators set about trying break the Catholic stranglehold on information by giving the Word of God to common people in their own language. Such men were hunted, tortured, strangled or burned. Men like Wycliffe, Hus, Zwingli, Calvin, Luther and Tyndale threatened the Catholic establishment and upon that moment, the Catholic mask slipped and the parasitical paganism of Rome within was revealed to be every bit as hostile towards Christians as it always had been. What Emperor Nero and his successors had done to those in centuries past, the Popes of these times would do again.

For example, in the 16th Century, Philip II sent the Duke of Alba to Flanders in Belgium to confiscate non-Latin Bibles and to rout out those who were reading the Word of God in their own language. The Inquisitors arrived in Bruges and found a non-Latin Bible while inspecting the house of the Mayor. One-by-one, family members were questioned, but every one claimed they knew nothing about how the Bible got into their house. Finally, a young maid-servant called Wrunken identified herself as the owner. The Mayor, knowing the penalty for her admission of guilt, tried to save her with a lie. *"Oh no, she only owns it. She doesn't ever read from it."* Wrunken refused to be defended by the lie and said, *"This book is mine. I am reading from it, and it is more precious to me than anything."* Wrunken was sentenced to die by suffocation. A hollow was made in the city wall, she was tied up inside, and then it was bricked up. This is typical of thousands of stories from that time.[8] Christians tortured and killed for their faith in God.

By the 20th Century, Communist revolutions were producing enmity towards Christians from atheistic regimes. Tyrants like Joseph Stalin and Mao Tse-tung believed Christians to be the biggest threat to their stranglehold on power. Therefore, churches were destroyed, Bibles were confiscated, pastors were killed and Christianity was banned. Indeed, the 20th Century saw more Christians martyred than all the previous centuries combined. Atheistic secular humanism perhaps turned out to be the most viciously intolerant worldview of them all.

The annual death toll continues to rise. Today, it's estimated that 165,000 Christians are martyred each year. Next year it will likely be more. The year after that, more still. Out of the 198 countries on earth, Christians are now at physical risk in 131 of them.[9] Rupert Shortt, in his Civitas report, Christianophobia, highlights several countries where persecution is particularly pronounced: Egypt, India, Iraq, Pakistan, Nigeria, Burma and China. However, he insists that the Middle East is the biggest problem declaring, *"there is now a serious risk that Christianity will disappear from its biblical heartlands."* This is mainly down to the rise of radical Islam, whose leaders have stoked a red hot hatred for Christianity.

This extremely brief overview of just a tiny portion of Christian persecution tells us that Jesus' warnings were well founded. From the moment he made his first disciple, persecution for following him has been absolutely standard. Today the threat to Christians comes from every conceivable angle. And this becomes all the more pertinent when we discover Jesus giving us another warning: That at the end of time, the persecution is not going to get better; it's going to get *worse*.

## END-TIME TRIBULATION

On the Mount of Olives, Jesus' disciples asked him what signs there would be to signal his return and the end of the world. Jesus' response has become known as the *Olivet Discourse*. This is how Matthew records it:

*"As Jesus was leaving the Temple grounds, his disciples pointed out to him the various Temple buildings. But he responded, "Do you see all these buildings? I tell you the truth, they will be*

*completely demolished. Not one stone will be left on top of another!"*

*Later, Jesus sat on the Mount of Olives. His disciples came to him privately and said, "Tell us, when will all this happen? What sign will signal your return and the end of the world?"*

*Jesus told them, "Don't let anyone mislead you, for many will come in my name, claiming, 'I am the Messiah.' They will deceive many. And you will hear of wars and threats of wars, but don't panic. Yes, these things must take place, but the end won't follow immediately. Nation will go to war against nation, and kingdom against kingdom. There will be famines and earthquakes in many parts of the world. But all this is only the first of the birth pains, with more to come.*

*"Then you will be arrested, persecuted, and killed. You will be hated all over the world because you are my followers. And many will turn away from me and betray and hate each other."* (Matthew 24:1-10)

The very first thing that Jesus tells his disciples to watch out for is an increase in false religion led by false Messiahs. John wrote, *"Dear children, the last hour is here. You have heard that the Antichrist is coming, and already many such antichrists have appeared. From this we know that the last hour has come."* (1 John 2:18) So prior to the appearance of the Antichrist, there will be many 'little' antichrists. This will be the first sign of his coming.

Jesus then says there will be an increase of war and threats of war. The geopolitical landscape will become increasingly tumultuous. There will also be an increase in famines and natural disasters. Jesus significantly describes all these problems as "birth pains". The significance of this metaphor is that birth pains increase in intensity and frequency as time rolls on. This is how it will be with all these things.

Next Jesus says, *"Then you will be arrested, persecuted, and killed. You will be hated all over the world because you are my followers. And many will turn away from me and betray and hate each other." (Matthew 24:10)*

How will this be a specific sign of the end? After all, if persecution has been normal throughout *all* history, it can hardly be can considered a sign just because it's still happening at the end. However, the specific sign Jesus is telling us about is that it will get noticeably *worse*. The birth pains metaphor applies. In fact, this is almost certainly describing a kind of end-time genocide. So bad will it be that many Christians will buckle under the pressure and for the sake of comfort, denounce their faith and join the crowd.

The news that Christianity is now the world's most persecuted religion isn't a surprise. The news that the persecution is increasing isn't a surprise. We are merely seeing the words of Jesus coming to life before our eyes. We are witnessing the birth pains. Do birth pains ever get easier? Not at all. As such, we must look to the future knowing that things aren't going to get easier; they're going to get worse.

Jesus continues on the Mount of Olives saying, *"And many false prophets will appear and will deceive many people. Sin will be rampant everywhere, and the love of many will grow cold. But the one who endures to the end will be saved. And the Good News about the Kingdom will be preached throughout the whole world, so that all nations will hear it; and then the end will come." (Matthew 24:11-14)*

We're going to need endurance in the end-times. Endurance right up until the end. Sin is going to be rampant. People will become more selfish. Love is going to grow cold. This isn't a pleasant picture.

Having given that general picture for the whole world, Jesus then focuses on the things that must occur specifically in Israel before the end comes:

*"The day is coming when you will see what Daniel the prophet spoke about—the sacrilegious object that causes desecration standing in the Holy Place." (Reader, pay attention!) "Then those in Judea must flee to the hills. A person out on the deck of a roof must not go down into the house to pack. A person out in the field must not return even to get a coat. How terrible it will be for pregnant women and for nursing mothers in those days. And pray that your flight will not be in winter or on the Sabbath. For there will be greater anguish than at any time since the world began. And it will never be so great again. In fact, unless that time of calamity is shortened, not a single person will survive. But it will be shortened for the sake of God's chosen ones." (Matthew 24:15-22)*

Jesus is describing an end-time event known as *Jacob's Trouble*, whereby Israel will be attacked and trampled upon during the reign of the Antichrist. This event was prophesied through the Old Testament prophets and Jesus can't return until it has happened. The Old Testament prophet Daniel especially, was given a lot of insight on this issue. He was told that the Antichrist would raise up an idolatrous statue on Temple Mount and that would be their cue to flee to the wilderness. Those who don't escape would be persecuted severely and killed. Jeremiah also prophesied about this day when he said:

*"I hear cries of fear;*
   *there is terror and no peace.*
*Now let me ask you a question:*
   *Do men give birth to babies?*
*Then why do they stand there, ashen-faced,*
   *hands pressed against their sides*
   *like a woman in labour?*
*In all history there has never been such a time of terror.*
   *It will be a time of trouble for my people Israel."*

(Jeremiah 30:5-7)

God tells Israel that their allies will desert them at this time: *"All your lovers—your allies—have left you and do not care about you anymore." (Jeremiah 30:14)*

Paul wrote to the Thessalonians about this time as well saying, *"When people are saying, "Everything is peaceful and secure," then disaster will fall on them as suddenly as a pregnant woman's labour pains begin. And there will be no escape."(1 Thessalonians 5:3)*

Notice how every single one of these verses about the end-times, and specifically Israel's trouble, mentions birth pains? This is not coincidence. Things are going to get *worse*. Jesus continues with more information saying:

*"Then if anyone tells you, 'Look, here is the Messiah,' or 'There he is,' don't believe it. For false messiahs and false prophets will*

*rise up and perform great signs and wonders so as to deceive, if possible, even God's chosen ones. See, I have warned you about this ahead of time.*

*"So if someone tells you, 'Look, the Messiah is out in the desert,' don't bother to go and look. Or, 'Look, he is hiding here,' don't believe it! For as the lightning flashes in the east and shines to the west, so it will be when the Son of Man comes. Just as the gathering of vultures shows there is a carcass nearby, so these signs indicate that the end is near." (Matthew 24:23-28)*

For a third time, Jesus warns us against the deception of false religion. Clearly, this is something he's very keen to stress. He tells us that when he returns, there won't be any doubt about it. The whole sky will light up like a  flash of lightning to herald his return.

Jesus then gives us a very important reference point. He says:

 *"Immediately **after** the anguish of those days,*

*the sun will be darkened,*
*   the moon will give no light,*
*the stars will fall from the sky,*
*   and the powers in the heavens will be shaken."*

*"**And then at last**, the sign that the Son of Man is coming will appear in the heavens, and there will be deep mourning among all the peoples of the earth. And they will see the Son of Man coming on the clouds of heaven with power and great glory. And he will send out his angels with the mighty blast of a trumpet, and they will gather his chosen ones from all over the world— from the farthest ends of the earth and heaven." (Matthew 24:29-31)*

I've emphasised the word "after" and the words "And then at last" because they are giving us a chronological timeline of events. *After* the increase in false religion, *after* all of the false prophets, *after* the increase in wars and threats of wars, *after* the increase in natural disasters and famines, *after* the persecution of Christians, *after* many of those Christians turn away from the faith, *after* the increase in sin which leads to hardened hearts and cynicism, *after* the sacrilegious idol is set up in Jerusalem....*after* all those things, the sun and moon will go dark and stars will fall from the sky, *and then at last*, Jesus comes to gather his chosen ones from all over the world.

Very simply the timeline that Jesus sets out for us is suffering and tribulation first *then* the sun and moon going dark and *then* 'at last' the rapture. There will be no rapture until after the tribulation and the sun and moon have gone dark.

That means that many of God's people will be here for the famines and natural disasters; they'll be here for the increase in false religion and false prophets; they'll be here for the increase in wars; they'll be here for the increase in persecution and hatred; they'll be here for a time of destruction for Jerusalem; they'll be here until the lights go down. No wonder Jesus says his followers will need endurance!

Will the Christian church go through tribulation during the end-times? This is the big question that everyone wants to know when they read Revelation. And that's why I have started our study here. I wanted to highlight that the Bible makes it clear that the church will *always* have tribulation - it's natural and maybe even necessary. History tells us that we have always *had* tribulation - it's never been any other way. Furthermore, the newspapers tell us that we currently *do* have tribulation - we already have it today. We are the most persecuted faith in the world. Right now. The Olivet Discourse simply tells us that it is going to get *worse*.

This is the sobering foundation that we must put in place as we turn to the book of Revelation itself.

# CHAPTER 2. THE THRONE ROOM (CHAPTER 4)

The future aspect of Revelation actually begins in Chapter 4. For that reason, that's where we will begin with our study. However, I don't intend to diminish the importance of the first three chapters in any way and so have included them as an Appendix to this book. You may want to read through them now before proceeding.

As Revelation begins, the year is around 95AD and John, the only one of Jesus' disciples who hasn't been martyred, is now an old man living in exile on the Greek island of Patmos. He introduces himself to us saying, *"I, John, am your brother and your partner in suffering and in God's Kingdom and in the patient endurance to which Jesus calls us. I was exiled to the island of Patmos for preaching the word of God and for my testimony about Jesus." (Rev 1:9)* Patmos is in the middle of the Aegean Sea and he has no means of leaving. Basically he's upset the authorities and has been placed under house-arrest there.

John makes it clear how this Revelation came to him on Patmos:

*"This is a revelation from Jesus Christ, which God gave him to show his servants the events that must soon take place. He sent an angel to present this revelation to his servant John, who faithfully reported everything he saw. This is his report of the word of God and the testimony of Jesus Christ.*

*God blesses the one who reads the words of this prophecy to the church, and he blesses all who listen to its message and obey what it says, for the time is near." (Rev 1:1-3)*

It *originated* with God, was *given* to his Son Jesus, was *delivered* by an angel to reveal it to John, who then *recorded* it faithfully with his own hand. We're then told that there is a blessing for those who read and obey what it says. As the only book in the Bible to offer such a blessing, we can deduce that Revelation is a special thing.

The angel who has been sent to John transports him in the spirit to heaven, where he finds himself in the throne room of God:

*"Then as I looked, I saw a door standing open in heaven, and the same voice I had heard before spoke to me like a trumpet blast. The voice said, "Come up here, and I will show you what must happen after this." And instantly I was in the Spirit..." (Rev 4:1-2)*

Upon his arrival there, John sees a scene so magnificent that it stretches his vocabulary to breaking point as he tries to describe it for us:

*"...and I saw a throne in heaven and someone sitting on it. The one sitting on the throne was as brilliant as gemstones—like jasper and carnelian. And the glow of an emerald circled his throne like a rainbow. Twenty-four thrones surrounded him, and twenty-four elders sat on them. They were all clothed in white and had gold crowns on their heads. From the throne came flashes of lightning and the rumble of thunder. And in front of the throne were seven torches with burning flames. This is the sevenfold Spirit of God. In front of the throne was a shiny sea of glass, sparkling like crystal." (Rev 4:2-6)*

John can only compare the throne room (and the one sitting on the throne) to the most spectacular and precious things that he knows. He uses lots of similes - the throne is *like* jasper and carnelian. There is a glow *like* a rainbow. These references to gemstones, rainbows and crystal are an attempt to portray the glory of what he is witnessing but in reality, no human language can do this scene justice. It's majesty, beauty and grandeur are beyond human description and comprehension.

However, having caught his breath, he starts to give us an idea of the layout of the throne room. He says, *"Twenty-four thrones surrounded him, and twenty-four elders sat on them. They were all clothed in white and had gold crowns on their heads." (Rev 4:4)* So the scene looks something like this:

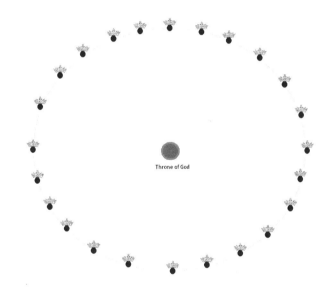

Throne of God

These twenty-four elders on thrones appear to be God's privy council. And although they aren't named, it's almost certain that they are angelic representatives of the two covenant peoples of God - Israel and the church. There were twelve tribes of Israel and twelve disciples of Christ so if we put them together we get the twenty-four. These two sets of twelve will remain precious to God forever. For evidence of that, we only need to flick to the end of Revelation where the new Jerusalem is being described: *"The city wall was broad and high, with twelve gates guarded by twelve angels. And the names of the twelve tribes of Israel were written on the gates. There were three gates on each side—east, north, south, and west. The wall of the city had twelve foundation stones, and on them were written the names of the twelve apostles of the Lamb." (Rev 21:12-14)* So the twelve gates of the new Jerusalem will each be named after a tribe of Israel and the twelve foundation stones of the city will each be inscribed with the names of Jesus' disciples. In this way, both these sets of twelve will be honoured for all eternity.

John describes the throne room further saying:

*"...in front of the throne were seven torches with burning flames. This is the sevenfold Spirit of God. In front of the throne was a shiny sea of glass, sparkling like crystal." (Rev 4:5-6)*

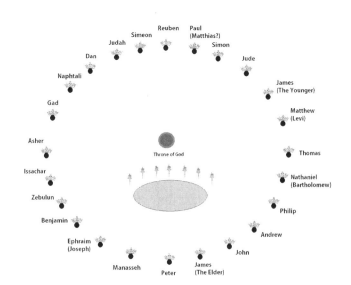

Next John says:

*"In the centre and around the throne were four living beings, each covered with eyes, front and back. The first of these living beings was like a lion; the second was like an ox; the third had a human face; and the fourth was like an eagle in flight. Each of these living beings had six wings, and their wings were covered all over with eyes, inside and out." (Rev 4:6-8)*

Our picture of the throne room now looks something like this:

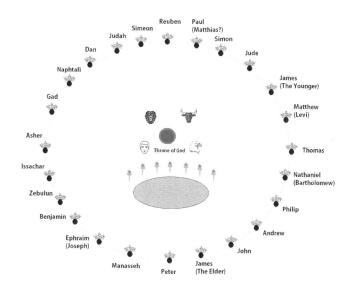

Many people have puzzled over who these four creatures are and what they represent. The Bible actually interprets itself though because they are identified in Ezekiel 10 as cherubim - a class of angel. In Ezekiel 10:14 it says, *"each of the four cherubim had four faces: the first was a face of an ox, the second was a human face, the third was the face of a lion, and*

*the fourth was the face of an eagle."* These are clearly the same beings.

Isaiah also confirms their identity when he says, *""O LORD of Heaven's Armies, God of Israel, you are enthroned between the mighty cherubim!" (Isaiah 37:16)*

Cherubim are often depicted today as harmless chubby babies floating around on Valentine's Day firing heart shaped arrows at lovers, but that image is very misleading. They are mighty angelic beings. On the other hand, it would also be misleading to believe they literally have four faces. The Bible is using vivid imagery here to convey to us the character of the cherubim. In other words, they have the strength of a lion, the service of an ox, the speed of an eagle and the intelligence of a man. The fact they have six wings suggests speed and their being covered in eyes also suggests deep or expansive perception.

Cherubim are one a few types of angels that the Bible informs us about. There are also seraphim and archangels for example. All these angels are assigned to carry out God's will but whenever cherubim are on the scene, it's normally to carry out God's orders of judgement. So rather than hearts and flowers, cherubim are more likely to bring with them discipline and punishment. And indeed, when they made their appearance back in Ezekiel, they were in the process of carrying out God's judgement against Israel.

What's interesting is that prior to carrying out that act of judgement it was written down on a scroll and given to the prophet. In Ezekiel 2 a voice from God says, *"Son of man, listen to what I say to you. Do not join them in their rebellion. Open your mouth, and eat what I give you."* Then I looked and saw a *hand reaching out to me. It held a scroll, which he unrolled. And I saw that both sides were covered with funeral songs, words of sorrow, and pronouncements of doom."(Ezekiel 2:8-10)* So God wrote down the pronouncements of doom against Israel on a scroll and gave it to his prophet before actually carrying it out.

The reason that's interesting is because exactly the same thing is going to happen here in Revelation.

## THE SCROLL

John looks at the throne of God he sees that He is holding a scroll:

*"Then I saw a scroll in the right hand of the one who was sitting on the throne. There was writing on the inside and the outside of the scroll, and it was sealed with seven seals." (Rev 5:1)*

Just like in Ezekiel's day, the scroll contains pronouncements of woe and doom. However, this time, it's not just for Israel; it's for the whole earth. Indeed, written on this scroll are God's orders for the end of human history as we know it. The whole world is about to be judged.

Unlike Ezekiel's scroll which was unrolled before him, this scroll is sealed shut with seven seals. In the first century it was extremely common practice for important documents to be written on scrolls and to be sealed shut with wax or clay in this way. Only a qualified person would be authorised to break the seals and read what was written within. Unfortunately, in this case, it appears as though nobody has such authority:

*"And I saw a strong angel, who shouted with a loud voice: "Who is worthy to break the seals on this scroll and open it?" But no one in heaven or on earth or under the earth was able to open the scroll and read it." (Rev 5:2-3)*

If the scroll can't be opened and the words within read, God's final judgement on wickedness and godlessness can't be proclaimed or enacted. This means that evil will continue unabated forever. Satan will remain the prince of the world. There will be no justice. All the murders, rapes, idolatry, thefts, genocides, lies, backstabbing, blasphemies and all the wickedness that this world has known can't be dealt with. The end can never come. It looks very much like the world has no hope of ever being put right. Will there be no justice? John weeps out of frustration:

*"Then I began to weep bitterly because no one was found worthy to open the scroll and read it." (Rev 5:4)*

However, all hope is *not* lost!

*"But one of the twenty-four elders said to me, "Stop weeping! Look, the Lion of the tribe of Judah, the heir to David's throne, has won the victory. He is worthy to open the scroll and its seven seals." (Rev 5:5)*

John looks around for a Lion but instead he sees a Lamb entering the throne room.

*"Then I saw a Lamb that looked as if it had been slaughtered, but it was now standing between the throne and the four living beings and among the twenty-four elders. He had seven horns and seven eyes, which represent the sevenfold Spirit of God that*

*is sent out into every part of the earth. He stepped forward and took the scroll from the right hand of the one sitting on the throne." (Rev 5:6-7)*

This Lamb that looks as though it has been slaughtered but yet lives, of course represents Jesus Christ. Jesus Christ is the Lion of the tribe of Judah; Jesus is the heir to David's throne; Jesus is the Lamb of God who was slain for the sins of the world and yet rose from the dead. Jesus is all those things. And Jesus is the only one who is qualified to judge the earth because he's the only one who walked on it, faced sin, was tempted as men are tempted, faced the same pressures that men face, and yet conquered it. In his perfect life, death and resurrection - in his victory - he has won the authority to judge us. He has felt the pain we feel, experienced the loneliness we experience, faced the same temptations we face, and yet remained sinless. It tells us a great deal about the fairness of God that we can only rightly be judged by someone who has walked in our shoes.

Indeed, while people instinctively believe Father God will judge them, the Bible tells us in several places that God has delegated this responsibility to his Son, Jesus. Jesus said, *"the Father judges no one. Instead, he has given the Son absolute authority to judge, so that everyone will honour the Son, just as they honour the Father. Anyone who does not honour the Son is certainly not honouring the Father who sent him." (John 5:22-23)* In other words, it's how we react to Jesus that will determine our fate. You may believe in God - so do demons - but what have you done with His Son?

Also notice that Jesus is portrayed as having seven horns and seven eyes. Horns represent power and seven is God's number of completeness. Therefore, the seven horns represent complete power. The seven eyes represent a complete depth of perception, knowledge and wisdom. He sees all, knows all and has absolute power and authority to judge the world.

Jesus takes the scroll from the Father on His throne and when he does so, the four cherubim and the twenty-four elders fall down in front of him and lead a worship session which resonates throughout all of heaven:

*"And when he took the scroll, the four living beings and the twenty-four elders fell down before the Lamb. Each one had a harp, and they held gold bowls filled with incense, which are the prayers of God's people. And they sang a new song with these words:*

*"You are worthy to take the scroll*
*    and break its seals and open it.*
*For you were slaughtered, and your blood has ransomed people for God*
*    from every tribe and language and people and nation.*
*And you have caused them to become*
*    a Kingdom of priests for our God.*
*    And they will reign on the earth."*

*Then I looked again, and I heard the voices of thousands and millions of angels around the throne and of the living beings and the elders. And they sang in a mighty chorus:*

*"Worthy is the Lamb who was slaughtered—*
*    to receive power and riches*
*and wisdom and strength*
*    and honour and glory and blessing."*

*And then I heard every creature in heaven and on earth and under the earth and in the sea. They sang:*

*"Blessing and honour and glory and power*
  *belong to the one sitting on the throne*
  *and to the Lamb forever and ever."*

*And the four living beings said, "Amen!" And the twenty-four elders fell down and worshiped the Lamb."(Rev 5:8-14)*

This is a hugely significant event. Whenever a mere angel or human is worshipped in the Bible, the object of the worship is always quick to put a stop to it and to make it clear that only God is worthy of such a thing.

Cornelius fell to his knees to worship Peter in Acts 10:25 and Peter instantly corrected him saying, *"Stand up! I'm a human being just like you!"*. At the end of Revelation, John falls down to worship the angel who had brought him the message and the angel says, *"No, don't worship me. I am a servant of God, just like you and your brothers the prophets, as well as all who obey what is written in this book. Worship only God!" (Rev 22:9)*

It's a clear principle throughout the Bible that no human, angel, saint or any other being should ever receive our worship - only God. So the fact that Jesus openly receives the worship of heaven, first by the cherubim and twenty-four elders, and then by the rest of the heavenly host - all thousands of millions of them - without protest, in the presence of God the Father, clearly tells us that Jesus himself is God; not an angel or mere human like so many false religions and cults have tried to suggest. He is truly worthy of our praise.

# CHAPTER 3.  THE SEVEN SEALS
## (THE GREAT TRIBULATION)

After the worship has ended, Jesus starts breaking each of the seven seals and with each seal that's broken, there is some kind of consequential turmoil for the earth. These painful birth pains, although increasing in frequency and intensity, are actually bringing us closer to the moment when the scroll can be opened and read, evil can be destroyed, God's justice can prevail, and goodness can be restored. The birth pains metaphor doesn't just tell us that bad things will happen; it tells us that there is something incredible on the other side.

As you read through the opening of the seals, you will also notice that the trouble each seal brings corresponds almost exactly to the trouble described by Jesus on the Mount of Olives in Matthew 24. All the same elements are there. False prophets, wars, natural disasters and persecution.

## THE FIRST SEAL

*"As I watched, the Lamb broke the first of the seven seals on the scroll. Then I heard one of the four living beings say with a voice like thunder, "Come!" I looked up and saw a white horse standing there. Its rider carried a bow, and a crown was placed on his head. He rode out to win many battles and gain the victory." (Rev 6:1-2)*

When the first seal is opened, one of the four cherubim calls forth a rider on a white horse who wears a crown and carries a bow. Don't expect a literal horseman to come out of the sky. In the same way that cherubim don't literally have four faces and in the same way Jesus isn't literally a Lamb, these are just vivid images to help us understand the spiritual happenings behind real world events. Indeed, for everything that happens in heaven, there is a corresponding event on the earth. This image of a white horse and rider, in fact, represents false religion and false prophets.

People commonly mistake it as a picture of Christ. It's easy to see why. There is a very explicit reference to Christ later in Revelation that describes him returning on a white horse:

*"Then I saw heaven opened, and a white horse was standing there. Its rider was named Faithful and True, for he judges fairly and wages a righteous war. His eyes were like flames of fire, and on his head were many crowns. A name was written on him that no one understood except himself. He wore a robe dipped in blood, and his title was the Word of God. The armies of heaven, dressed in the finest of pure white linen, followed him on white horses. From his mouth came a sharp sword to strike down the nations. He will rule them with an iron rod. He will release the fierce wrath of God, the Almighty, like juice flowing from a winepress. On his robe at his thigh was written this title: King of all kings and Lord of all lords."(Rev 19:11-16)*

But while there are definite similarities between this clear reference to Christ and the first seal rider on the white horse, they're not the same. For example, the first seal rider has one crown whereas Jesus has many crowns - he is the King of kings and the Lord of lords. Also, this rider carries a bow whereas Jesus strikes the nations with a sword. So the first seal rider looks like Christ...but he's not Christ. He's an impostor!

Could he then be the Antichrist? This is probably the most common misinterpretation. However, the Antichrist doesn't make his entrance until Revelation 13, many chapters later, and much further along the timeline.

This rider isn't the Christ and he's not *the* Antichrist. It's an image of the *many* false messiahs, *many* false prophets and the rise of false religion that *precede* the Antichrist. Remember John wrote, *"Dear children, the last hour is here. You have heard that the Antichrist is coming, and already many such antichrists have appeared. From this we know that the last hour has come." (1 John 2:18)* In other words, we know the last days of earth are coming primarily because there will be a rise in false religion and false prophets. And these will *precede* the coming of the Antichrist himself. Remember when the disciples asked Jesus *"What sign will signal your return and the end of the world?"* the very first sign he talked about was, *"Don't let anyone mislead you, for many will come in my name, claiming, 'I am the Messiah.' They will deceive many."* So the very first sign of the end will be a proliferation of false religion. This first rider represents that fact. He represents a *concept* rather than an individual (just as the subsequent three horsemen do).

Jesus and Revelation agree on the levels of success these many false prophets will enjoy. Revelation says this rider will win many victories and Jesus says these false prophets will deceive many. The fact the rider wears a crown signifies that these antichrists will gain much prestige and honour. A lot of people are going to be led astray. This will all increase towards the end.

What constitutes an 'antichrist'? The Bible tells us *"Anyone who says that Jesus is not the Christ. Anyone who denies the Father and the Son is an antichrist. Anyone who denies the Son doesn't have the Father, either. But anyone who acknowledges the Son has the Father also." (1 John 2:22-23)*

An antichrist is anyone who denies that Jesus is the Christ. Anyone who denies he is the Son of God. Anyone who denies he is the Messiah. Again, it's our reaction to the Son that's important.

Charles Taze Russell, founder of the Jehovah's Witnesses, denied the deity of Jesus and therefore, he was an antichrist by the Biblical definition. Sun Myung Moon, founder of the Universal Church (Moonies), denied the deity of Jesus and therefore, he was an antichrist by the Biblical definition. He joins Joseph Smith (founder of the Mormons), Mary Baker Eddy (Christian Science), Dr John Thomas (Christadelphians), Herbert W Armstrong (Armstrongism/Worldwide Church of God) and Charles and Myrtle Fillmore (Unity School of Christianity) amongst others. These are people who came in Jesus' name but yet were deceivers.

And then there are the likes of L Ron Hubbard (Scientology), Muhammad (Islam), Buddha (Buddhism), Guru Nanak (Sikhism) and indeed, founders, leaders and prophets of *all* religions and cults who have drawn people away from the truth about Christ. This even includes the recent proliferation of New Age leaders who have led people into the occult and Eastern mysticism. We could also put in this bracket the prophets of Atheism such as Charles Darwin, Richard Dawkins, Sam Harris and Stephen Hawking. These are people who deny, or even vehemently attack Christ, whilst establishing the faith-based, man-centred philosophy of Secular Humanism.

We can clearly see the rise of false religion in our world today through such people. The world is increasingly turning their backs on Christ and embracing this occultism, Eastern mysticism, secular humanism and New Age spirituality. Don't be disheartened that this is happening and think that God has lost control. These things must happen.[1]

## THE SECOND SEAL

*"When the Lamb broke the second seal, I heard the second living being say, "Come!" Then another horse appeared, a red one. Its rider was given a mighty sword and the authority to take peace from the earth. And there was war and slaughter everywhere."* (Rev 6:3-4)

When the second seal is opened, another of the four cherubim calls forth a rider on a red horse. Again, this is just a spiritual image; don't expect a red horse to come out of the sky. The red horse represents a pronounced increase in war all over the earth. The geopolitical situation will become increasingly unstable.

According to a 2011 study conducted by Professor Mark Harrison from the University of Warwick and Nikolas Wolf from Humboldt University, the frequency of wars between states increased at a rate of 2% each year on average between 1870 and 2001. Harrison says, *"The number of conflicts has been rising on a stable trend. Because of two world wars, the pattern is obviously disturbed between 1914 and 1945 but remarkably, after 1945 the frequency of wars resumed its upward course on pretty much the same path as before 1913."*[2]

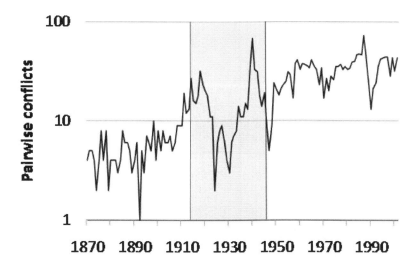

As the birth pains increase in frequency and intensity, we will see this trend continue.

## THE THIRD SEAL

*"When the Lamb broke the third seal, I heard the third living being say, "Come!" I looked up and saw a black horse, and its rider was holding a pair of scales in his hand. And I heard a voice from among the four living beings say, "A loaf of wheat bread or three loaves of barley will cost a day's pay. And don't waste the olive oil and wine." (Rev 6:5-6)*

When the third seal is opened, the third cherubim calls forth a rider on a black horse. This image represents economic collapse and hyper-inflation which leads to famine. We've already seen this dynamic in action during the 2008 financial crisis. Previously comfortable families were plunged into poverty and began struggling to pay for food. For example, the Trussell Trust reported that UK food bank use rose by 170% in 2013.[3] In the

United States, Gleaners Indianna Food Bank reported that 50 million Americans - that's 1 in 6 - were experiencing 'food insecurity' in 2012.[4]

The Bible tells us that the world's economy is going to become increasingly unstable and will suffer an even bigger collapse in the future. This will lead to a period of still worse financial turmoil. When we consider that national debts are now so astronomical that they can never be paid back and are increasing by the second, we begin to understand that the whole world is sitting on an economic time bomb. In fact, if you go to www.nationaldebtclocks.org, you can watch world debt rising in real time. When this financial collapse takes hold, it will cost a whole day's wages just to buy one loaf of wheat bread. Barley will be slightly less affected but even so, one day's wages will only buy *three* barley loaves. People are going to be struggling just to survive.

There's an interesting nuance to this passage that's worth pointing out. It says, *"A loaf of wheat bread or three loaves of barley will cost a day's wages **but don't harm the olive oil and wine"**.* Bread is a cheap, dietary staple. However, olive oil and wine represent expensive, luxury items. And it seems they won't be touched by the crisis.

What the Bible appears to suggest here is that the inflation and food shortages will be an issue for the middle and working class folks only, but it will have almost no impact on the rich. We saw this dynamic in the aftermath of 2008 too. While many working people lost their homes and fell into poverty in the years following the collapse, and while tax hikes squeezed the middle classes to breaking point, manufacturers and retailers of prestige brands and luxury goods actually reported *increased* sales figures. In other words, the super rich were continuing to spend freely. The financial crisis hadn't caused them *any* discomfort. This has been the way throughout all history. When there is a rising tide of financial insecurity, the yachts are lifted but the peasants drown. What we are witnessing today, and what will continue to occur in future, is a widening gap between rich and poor.

## THE FOURTH SEAL

*"When the Lamb broke the fourth seal, I heard the fourth living being say, "Come!" I looked up and saw a horse whose colour was pale green. Its rider was named Death, and his companion was the Grave. These two were given authority over one-fourth of the earth, to kill with the sword and famine and disease and wild animals." (Rev 6:7-8)*

When the fourth seal is opened, the last cherubim calls forth a pale green horse - an image that represents death. Thankfully I've never seen a dead body in the flesh but I'm told that this is the colour that corpses turn. In other words, as a result of all this war, economic troubles, famine, diseases and natural disasters, death will inevitably follow hard on the heels of those things. When it says *"These two were given authority over one-fourth of the earth"*, this is often interpreted as, "a quarter of the planet's population will die." It may not mean that. It could just mean - and I think this is the more likely explanation - that a quarter of the earth's *geographical* area is going to be particularly badly affected. Like the Middle East, for example.

## COMPARING THE FIRST FOUR SEALS WITH THE OLIVET DISCOURSE

To see just how the Olivet Discourse and the first four seals of Revelation mirror each other, it might be helpful if we put them side-by-side.

| OLIVET DISCOURSE (Matthew 24) | THE FIRST FOUR SEALS (Revelation 6) |
|---|---|
| Later, Jesus sat on the Mount of Olives. His disciples came to him privately and said, "Tell us, when will all this happen? What sign will signal your return and the end of the world?"<br><br>Jesus told them, "Don't let anyone mislead you, for many will come in my name, claiming, 'I am the Messiah.' They will deceive many. - Matt 24:4-5 | FIRST SEAL (False Religion)<br>As I watched, the Lamb broke the first of the seven seals on the scroll. Then I heard one of the four living beings say with a voice like thunder, "Come!" I looked up and saw a white horse standing there. Its rider carried a bow, and a crown was placed on his head. He rode out to win many battles and gain the victory. - Revelation 6:1-2 |
| And you will hear of wars and threats of wars, but don't panic. Yes, these things must take place, but the end won't follow immediately. Nation will go to war against nation, and kingdom against kingdom. - Matt 24:6-7a | SECOND SEAL (Wars)<br>When the Lamb broke the second seal, I heard the second living being say, "Come!" Then another horse appeared, a red one. Its rider was given a mighty sword and the authority to take peace from the earth. And there was war and slaughter everywhere. - Revelation 6:3-4 |
| There will be famines and earthquakes in many parts of the world. But all this is only the first of the birth pains, with more to come. - Matt 24:7b-8 | THIRD SEAL (Economic Crises & Famine)<br>When the Lamb broke the third seal, I heard the third living being say, "Come!" I looked up and saw a black horse, and its rider was holding a pair of scales in his hand. And I heard a voice from among the four living beings say, "A loaf of |

| | wheat bread or three loaves of barley will cost a day's pay. And don't waste the olive oil and wine." - Revelation 6:5-6 |
|---|---|
| "Then you will be arrested, persecuted, and killed. You will be hated all over the world because you are my followers. And many will turn away from me and betray and hate each other. And many false prophets will appear and will deceive many people. Sin will be rampant everywhere, and the love of many will grow cold. But the one who endures to the end will be saved. And the Good News about the Kingdom will be preached throughout the whole world, so that all nations will hear it; and then the end will come. - Matt 24:9-14 | FOURTH SEAL (Death) When the Lamb broke the fourth seal, I heard the fourth living being say, "Come!" I looked up and saw a horse whose colour was pale green. Its rider was named Death, and his companion was the Grave. These two were given authority over one-fourth of the earth, to kill with the sword and famine and disease and wild animals. - Rev 6:7-8 |

There seems to be quite a clear correlation between the two passages. And if it's a valid comparison to make, we should also note that around the third seal, marked by economic collapse and famine, Jesus tells us that there will also be an increase in natural disasters. Here is a graph from the International Disaster Database that illustrates how this is happening right now.[5]

Natural disasters reported 1900 - 2011

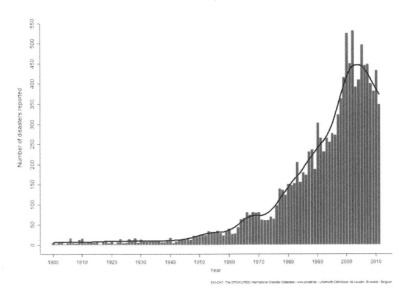

Scientists warn that this trend is going to continue in the years ahead, attributing the phenomenon to man-made climate change. While the theory of man-made climate change is debatable, the Bible makes it clear that they're right to predict increased volatility in the natural world. Every time you turn on the news and see a tsunami, a flood, an earthquake or a hurricane causing devastation in some part of the world, you're actually witnessing the fulfilment of Biblical prophecy.

And that raises an important question. Where exactly are we in the prophecy timeline?

## WHERE ARE WE?

We've seen there will be an increase in false prophets and religion...and that's already happening; we've seen there will be an increase in wars...and that's already happening; we've seen there will be an increase in economic crises, food poverty and wealth disparity...and that's already happening, and we've seen there will be an increase in natural disasters and disease...and that's already happening. With this in mind, I believe we can legitimately entertain the idea that the first four seals have *already* been opened and we're *already* experiencing the beginning of the birth pains. The news channels seems to confirm this with every passing day.

Many people want to know where we are in the timeline of events and how long we have to wait until Jesus returns. No one can answer that question accurately. However, Jesus told us that we would be able to discern when the time was *approaching* saying, *"Now learn a lesson from the fig tree. When its branches bud and its leaves begin to sprout, you know that summer is near. In the same way, when you see all these things, you can know his return is very near, right at the door."(Matt 24:32-33)* Since we can indeed observe *"all these things"* happening in our world right now, we might not be at the end, but we can say with a certain degree of confidence that we're at the *beginning* of the end. And although we don't know how long the birth pains will last, we can say with some justification that they've *begun.* That should focus our minds as we consider how to live in the times ahead.

## A CHRISTIAN GENOCIDE?

When the fourth seal is broken and there is an increase in death in the world, it appears as though that's especially going to be true for Christians. Jesus says during the Olivet Discourse, *"Then you will be arrested, persecuted, and killed. You will be hated all over the world because you are my followers."* As we've already noted, while that has always been true; while Christians have *always* been hated, persecuted and martyred for their faith throughout history, there will be a noticeable increase towards the end.

In the same way that there have always been false prophets but they will increase; in the same way there have always been wars but they will increase; in the same way there has often been financial difficulty and famine but it will increase; in the same way that there have always been natural disasters but they will increase; there has always been persecution for Christians...but it's going to increase. Significantly. In fact, Jesus may even be describing a kind of genocide here.

Earlier I quoted The International Society for Human Rights - the secular observatory based in Frankfurt, Germany, who said that 80% of all acts of religious discrimination in the world today are now directed at Christians. Statistically speaking, that already makes Christians by far the most persecuted religious body on the planet. Right now. Today.

The Spectator recently published an article which said, *"In effect, the world is witnessing the rise of an entire new generation of Christian martyrs. The carnage is occurring on such a vast scale that it represents not only the most dramatic Christian story of our time, but arguably the premier human rights challenge of this era as well."*[6]

Even places which were relatively safe for Christians are now becoming dangerous. In Iraq, Christians numbered 1.5 million in 1991. Today, it's estimated that their number is closer to 150,000. That represents a 90% decrease in just over 20 years. No wonder some experts are predicting the extinction of Christianity from the Middle East. In Africa, reports of Islamic militants breaking into homes and telling people to convert or die are becoming common. A woman named Florence reported the exact words of her attackers in Nigeria: *"We have been telling you people [Christians] to convert to Islam but you people refuse. So the only thing is to get rid of all of you and to inherit all that you have. If you women will not convert to Islam and marry us, we will kill all of you and your children."*[7] Christians are being chased, hounded, persecuted and killed in increasing numbers all over the world. This is a catastrophe of Biblical proportions...literally!

Even in the West, we're seeing a noticeable rise in anti-Christian/anti-Christ sentiment. Reports are coming through with increasing regularity of home churches being shut down, street preachers being jailed under hate speech charges for saying that Jesus Christ is Lord, Christian business owners being targeted for opposing homosexuality, and all mentions of God being removed from schools and halls of government. Right now the persecution hasn't led to waves of martyrdom or even much physical violence, but just as Nero's persecution began small - confiscation of property, illegalisation of the faith, imprisonment - and escalated, that's how waves of persecution generally begin. Anyone who has studied German attitudes towards the Jews in the 1930s will know that this is exactly how the holocaust began too. At first it was just a whispering campaign, verbal abuse, then boycotts on Jewish businesses, confiscation of property and vandalization of homes. Before long, they were being blamed for all society's ills (just as Nero had blamed Christians for all Rome's) and they were being carted off to concentration camps and gas chambers.

We must not be complacent. Antichristian sentiment will certainly increase and get more severe as we get closer to the time of *the* Antichrist himself.

Jesus says that many will buckle under the increasing pressure of this hatred from the world and will renounce their faith for the sake of comfort. He says, *"many will turn away from me and betray and hate each other."*

Others will leave Christ to follow the proliferation of false prophets who will tickle their ears with promises of an easier life. Sin will increase. Immorality will increase. Christians will increasingly stand out, be excluded and looked down upon. It's going to take an increasing amount of courage to stand up for Jesus in the world. However, Jesus says that those "who endure to the end will be saved." (Matt 24:13)

He doesn't mean that they will necessarily have their earthly lives spared - just that they will gain everlasting life for their faithfulness to him, even to the point of death. Obviously this means that the cowards who capitulate and do *not* endure to the end, will *not* be saved. I'll repeat what I said in *"Stay Free"*, it is possible to renounce your faith, walk away, and forfeit your salvation. We must endure.

Now all this persecution and killing of Christians should help us understand the next seal in the sequence....

## THE FIFTH SEAL

*"When the Lamb broke the fifth seal, I saw under the altar the souls of all who had been martyred for the word of God and for being faithful in their testimony. They shouted to the Lord and said, "O Sovereign Lord, holy and true, how long before you judge the people who belong to this world and avenge our blood for what they have done to us?" Then a white robe was given to each of them. And they were told to rest a little longer until the full number of their brothers and sisters—their fellow servants*

*of Jesus who were to be martyred—had joined them." (Rev 6:9-11)*

Here we see the souls of the martyred Christians filling up heaven. This lends weight to the theory that the rise in antichrist sentiment will eventually lead to a genocide - the tribulation of the last days will culminate in a "Great Tribulation" of martyrdom for the church. Since the fourth seal, which brought the rider called Death, affected only a fourth of the earth, this *probably* isn't a global genocide, but certainly it will affect a large part of the planet. This may even describe the virtual extinction of Christianity from the Middle East that some suggest has already begun. It's certainly in-keeping with the Spectator article that suggests a new wave of Christian martyrdom has started there. At any rate, we shouldn't be complacent, believing this will only affect our Middle Eastern brothers and sisters. We may all be asked to lay down our lives for the name of Christ in the years to come. It would do us good to prepare for this sobering eventuality. And to pray for those who are already suffering.

John describes the martyrs in heaven shouting out to the Lord to give them justice. They ask him how long it will be before he pours out his judgement on their murderers. However, there are still two more seals to break before the scroll can be opened and God's wrath can be read and enacted. The martyred souls are given white robes (which will help us identify them later) and are told to wait just a little while longer.

## THE SIXTH SEAL

*"I watched as the Lamb broke the sixth seal, and there was a great earthquake. The sun became as dark as black cloth, and*

*the moon became as red as blood. Then the stars of the sky fell to the earth like green figs falling from a tree shaken by a strong wind. The sky was rolled up like a scroll, and all of the mountains and islands were moved from their places.*

*Then everyone—the kings of the earth, the rulers, the generals, the wealthy, the powerful, and every slave and free person—all hid themselves in the caves and among the rocks of the mountains. And they cried to the mountains and the rocks, "Fall on us and hide us from the face of the one who sits on the throne and from the wrath of the Lamb. For the great day of their wrath has come, and who is able to survive?" (Rev 6:12-17)*

When the sixth seal is broken the sun goes dark, the moon turns blood-red and the stars fall from the sky. This heralds the beginning of the Day of Wrath.

John describes the scene in heaven at this time:

*"After this I saw a vast crowd, too great to count, from every nation and tribe and people and language, standing in front of the throne and before the Lamb. They were clothed in white robes and held palm branches in their hands. And they were shouting with a great roar,*

*"Salvation comes from our God who sits on the throne*
*and from the Lamb!"*

*And all the angels were standing around the throne and around the elders and the four living beings. And they fell before the throne with their faces to the ground and worshiped God. They sang,*

*"Amen! Blessing and glory and wisdom*
*and thanksgiving and honour*
*and power and strength belong to our God*
*forever and ever! Amen."*

*Then one of the twenty-four elders asked me, "Who are these*
*who are clothed in white? Where did they come from?"*

*And I said to him, "Sir, you are the one who knows."*

*Then he said to me, "These are the ones who died in the great*
*tribulation. They have washed their robes in the blood of the*
*Lamb and made them white.*

*"That is why they stand in front of God's throne*
*and serve him day and night in his Temple.*
*And he who sits on the throne*
*will give them shelter.*
*They will never again be hungry or thirsty;*
*they will never be scorched by the heat of the sun.*
*For the Lamb on the throne*
*will be their Shepherd.*
*He will lead them to springs of life-giving water.*
*And God will wipe every tear from their eyes."*

*(Rev 7:9-17)*

Heaven is being flooded with martyrs, identifiable by their white
robes. One of the twenty-four elders asks John if he can guess
who they are, and really John should have known because he'd
seen them being given their white robes during the fifth seal,
but John basically says, "you know better than I do." So the

elder confirms *"These are the ones who died in the great tribulation."* Since they have died in the great tribulation, it's simple logic to deduce they must have gone through it.

Indeed, the church has been on earth for *all* the seals. It's been around to witness the rise in false prophets and false religion (first seal), it's been here for the increase in wars (second seal), it's been here for the economic collapse, famines and natural disasters (third seal), it's witnessed an increase in contagious diseases and death (fourth seal) and a time of great persecution and martyrdom (fifth seal) - a time which saw many of them executed. In other words, there will be no secret rapture before any of those things takes place. The church *will* go through the tribulation described until this point.

Indeed, we get a sense in this passage that although the church has just been through some truly terrible times and has suffered greatly through hunger, thirst, lack of shelter and although they have cried many tears, they're now full of relief and jubilation because it's finally over. They're in heaven now. They're safe. They will never suffer again. The feeling of joy is almost palpable. There's a buzz of excitement and an eruption of worship in heaven as they rejoice and worship God. Clearly they are also anticipating the vengeance that God is going to pour out on their tormentors and murderers. And that day of wrath is close now - there is just one more seal to open.

## THE PRE-TRIBULATION RAPTURE THEORY

Before we go on to look at the opening of the final seal, we have to pause to address a grave error that has infiltrated the church.

You see, despite these explicit passages in Revelation that clearly state, *"These are the ones who died in the great tribulation";* despite all the warnings from Jesus that tribulation would be a natural consequence of following him; despite the fact that he was persecuted and crucified himself and said no servant is greater than the Master; despite the warnings from Paul and Peter that tribulation would come to the godly; despite the fact that all the disciples except one were persecuted and martyred; despite the fact that persecution and martyrdom has been the norm for Christians for 2,000 years; despite the fact that more people are dying for their faith today than at any time in human history; despite the fact that a new wave of martyrdom is sweeping the Middle East to such a degree that it's threatening to extinguish the light of the church from that region, the vast majority of the Western church has been brought up to believe that they *won't* go through the great tribulation.

They hold to something known as the "Pre-Tribulation Rapture Theory".

This theory basically states that the Christian church will be secretly pulled out of the world before any of the things we've been hearing about happens. In other words, before any of the first six seals are opened or before anything in the Olivet Discourse takes place.

In fact, the Western church is absolutely offended at the idea that God may ask them to suffer for His name. "How could God possibly allow that to happen to *us*?", we think. My question is, since tribulation has been promised to the church and since it's been the norm for everyone else throughout history, what makes us think he *won't* allow it to happen to us? Why do we think we're unique? The Bible clearly says, *"...we **must** suffer many hardships to enter the Kingdom of God."(Acts 14:22)(emphasis added)* Why do we think that statement doesn't apply to us?

The history of the Pre-Trib theory is an interesting one.

Up until 1830, no Christian believed that they would escape the great tribulation. The Pre-Tribulation Rapture theory had simply not been heard of.

The first person to promote it as a concept was a man called John Nelson Darby. Darby was an Anglo-Irish evangelist who developed a reputation as an expert on Biblical prophecy in the 1830s and 1840s. During these years he preached and gave lectures around Britain and Europe - the most significant of these lectures being a series of eleven in Geneva, Switzerland, collectively titled, "The Hope of the Church." The hope Darby expressed was that the church would be spared the horrors of the great tribulation.

Despite a complete absence of Biblical evidence to support his hope, Darby's ideas nevertheless gained widespread acceptance in the 19th Century. The pivotal moment in the theory's popularisation, however, came in the early 20th Century, when they were picked up by Cyrus Ingerson Scofield. Scofield was the author of the Scofield Reference Bible, which was revolutionary for its time in the sense that it was the first to include a commentary of references and footnotes alongside the Biblical text. First published in 1909 and then updated in 1917, it was in this commentary that Scofield perpetuated Darby's ideas of a Pre-Tribulation rapture. As his Bible became one of the most widely circulated Bibles of its era, suddenly the whole theory began to spread like wildfire. By the end of World

War II, it's estimated that two million copies had been sold. Even today, Scofield's Reference Bible is consistently reported to be one of the best selling Bibles in the United Kingdom.

Not only did Scofield's commentary influence the common man directly, but it found its way into seminaries too. Today, many of the largest and most influential seminaries in the world teach the Pre-Trib theory because of the influence of Scofield's Bible, which sits on the study shelves of professors and lecturers. Consequently, many of the pastors who have gone through those seminaries now teach their congregations the Pre-Trib theory, just as they were taught by their professors before. Some of those pastors have TV and media ministries as well. Therefore, they are able to broadcast their thoughts about a Pre-Trib theory into millions of homes around the world every day. In fact, so prevalent is the Pre-Trib theory today that it is extremely rare to find a pastor with a TV and media ministry who does *not* espouse it. It has become the standardised method by which the end-times are understood.

The theory's ideas have entered public consciousness by another media stream too. In the 1970s, a series of films produced by Russell S Doughton promoted the idea that a pre-tribulation rapture could happen at any moment. This series, often collectively called "The Rapture Series", began with "A Thief In The Night" - a story of a young girl called Patty Myers who wakes up one day to find that her husband and millions of others have suddenly disappeared without trace. This sensational dramatisation caught the public's imagination and it was updated somewhat in the 1990s through Tim LaHaye's "Left Behind" series which has spawned movies, books, graphic novels, albums and even video games. In other words, the snowball of an idea that began with Darby in the 1830s had turned into an avalanche by the 1990s.

Today, millions of Christians hold to the pre-tribulation theory because of these influences. If you were to ask them to coherently explain why they believe in a pre-tribulation rapture, the majority couldn't, because it's not a conclusion they have reached with their own minds - they are simply repeating what they have heard many pastors preach.

It's easy to see why such a theory would become so popular. Who honestly wants to hear that we'll be on earth to witness an increase in false religion, war, natural disasters, economic crises, famine and disease? Who relishes the idea that we'll be beaten up, thrown into prison and executed? We'd much rather like to think that God will pull us up into heaven without any trouble befalling us. We'd much rather be kicking back on our hammocks in heaven while all this suffering is taking place. Therefore, anyone who can tell us what we want to hear and back it up with some kind of Biblical reasoning, no matter how contrived and convoluted, will have our attention. And there have been many who have lined up to try. They move chapters around, re-arrange the Biblical timeline, pluck verses out of context and misinterpret others in order to get the Bible to fit with their preconceived notion. Then they present the confused results to audiences around the world who don't really understand entirely what's been said but grasp onto the general idea because it's what they want to believe.

We're especially prone to this self-deception in the Western Church.

Because the truth is, although suffering has been the norm for the vast majority of the church around the world for 2000 years and therefore, our brothers and sisters in those far-off places have not flinched when told they would be expected to suffer some more at the end of the age, the *Western* church has rarely been asked to suffer at all. Therefore, although suffering has always been very normal for *other* Christians, it's very abnormal for *us*. Just the idea of suffering for God is rather alien in this part of the world. We've existed within a safe bubble of religious liberty since at least the 1800s. We've been able to worship freely. We've been able to pray, read the Bible, gather together and speak freely in the name of Christ. In fact, for a while there, due to some notable revivals that swept the US and UK in the 19th Century, Christians were in the *majority* in the West. Churches all over the land were packed out every Sunday.

In other words, during our recent history, the theme of being persecuted for following Christ, which is so prevalent in the Bible, became detached from our every-day experience. In reality we lived in comfort. In reality we had become wealthy. That cosy social and religious environment afforded us the opportunity to develop a theology that pandered to our lust for more of those things. Preachers began telling us that God would never want us to suffer. Instead, they said that God wanted us to be even more comfortable, to live a life of even greater ease, and to increase constantly in health, wealth and happiness. The prosperity gospel took hold. We built plush sanctuaries with air conditioning and comfortable chairs. The preachers told us that God wanted us to have that new car, that job promotion, that house extension and that gold watch. In contrast to the greats of the faith who were cited in Hebrews as willingly suffering torture because they had *"placed their hope in a better life after the resurrection"*[8], Western pastors said that God wanted you to have "Your Best Life Now."[9] And then they told us that after our life of ease, God would rapture us out of the earth before things got too tricky. We lap this stuff up because it's exactly what we hope to be true. If it were possible for us to write the script that's exactly how most of us would write it. It's what the Bible calls, "ear-tickling" preaching (2 Tim 4:3-4).

It's true that the Western church hasn't been totally unaware of church persecution throughout these years. We've often heard missionary reports of problems in Asia and Africa...but that's Asia and Africa...we still find it difficult to believe that it could be God's will for *us*. The thought that we will go through the great tribulation is basically horrifying and we simply don't want to believe it. A large number of people are therefore clinging to the Pre-Trib theory out of a baseless hope rather than a Biblical reality.

**Quite simply, there is no Biblical support for a Pre-Tribulation rapture of the church.**

Whenever you speak to a "Pre-Tribber" about this issue, the one verse that they will nearly always reach for to defend the theory is this one from Thessalonians: *"...for God hath not appointed us unto wrath." (1 Thess 5:9)(KJV)*

"There you go", they say. "We will not experience God's wrath. Case closed."

The problem is that the great tribulation that came with the opening of the first six seals - those troubles described in the Olivet Discourse - that *wasn't* God's wrath. The pronouncements of God's wrath are written on the scroll but the scroll hasn't been opened yet.

The tribulation and martyrdom of the church during the seals merely comes at the hands of wicked, godless people who are sliding deeper into immorality and hatred for Christ; *not* at the hands of God. The tribulation of the seals are a *precursor* to the Day of Wrath. Let's recap what happens after the sixth seal is broken and the sun and moon are darkened:

*"I watched as the Lamb broke the sixth seal, and there was a great earthquake. The sun became as dark as black cloth, and the moon became as red as blood. Then the stars of the sky fell to the earth like green figs falling from a tree shaken by a strong wind. The sky was rolled up like a scroll, and all of the mountains and islands were moved from their places.*

*Then everyone—the kings of the earth, the rulers, the generals, the wealthy, the powerful, and every slave and free person—all hid themselves in the caves and among the rocks of the mountains. And they cried to the mountains and the rocks, "Fall on us and hide us from the face of the one who sits on the throne and from the wrath of the Lamb. **For the great day of their wrath has come**, and who is able to survive?" (Rev 6:12-17) (emphasis added)*

The great day of God's wrath comes *after* the seals have been broken and *after* the lights have gone off.

Joel confirms the sequence for us too saying, *"The sun will become dark, and the moon will turn blood red **before** that great and terrible day of the LORD arrives." (Joel 2:31)(emphasis added)*

The sun being darkened and moon turning blood red marks the transition from the Tribulation to the Day of Wrath. So while there is a good case to be made for the church leaving before the Day of Wrath comes, we are certainly here *until* that moment. There is no cause to believe that we'll be absent for the opening of the six seals. Indeed, as I suggested earlier, we're already seeing the beginnings of the effects of those six seals.

How will the church be removed from the earth before the Day of Wrath? Well, unfortunately it seems that many will have left through martyrdom. That's the plain message from the fifth seal. Another explicit reason for the absence of the church after this point is that many will have buckled under the pressure of the persecution and betrayed Christ. Paul wrote about a great falling away of the church prior to the appearance of the Antichrist saying, *"Let no man deceive you by any means: for that day shall not come, except there come a falling away first." (2 Thess 2:3)(KJV)* There are no figures placed on that falling away but I think it might be larger than we imagine. It will be revealed that many who called themselves Christians were only nominally so, or not at all. Can the church's absence after this point also be partly explained by a *Pre-Wrath* rapture? Possibly. The more I study the issue, the more I tend to think not. But let's leave it open as an option for now and return to the idea later on.

However the church leaves, it seems clear that it has pretty much happened by the sixth seal. Revelation switches its focus so noticeably at this point that it will hardly mention the church again. It's a bit like the Book of Acts in reverse. Acts starts by telling the story of the believers in Israel but around chapter 9 there's a gear change and the focus switches entirely to Paul's ministry to the Gentiles. This signifies the rejection of the Gospel by the Jews and the beginning of the "Church Age" or the "Age of the Gentiles". In Revelation, this works in reverse. It starts with a focus on the Gentile church (the first three chapters of Revelation are letters to the Gentile churches) but then around the sixth or seventh seal, attention reverts back to Israel.

Before we look at that in more depth, it's worth pointing out that the most common mistake that people make with this whole rapture issue is rooted in simple terminology. You see, most people will use the phrase "Great Tribulation" as a blanket term for the whole of Revelation. I guess it's easy to see why... most of Revelation talks about trouble of some kind. Indeed, peace doesn't break out until the very last two chapters. However, to be strictly accurate with our terminology, we must recognise that the Great Tribulation actually ends with the opening of the seventh seal. Once the final seal has been opened, we then switch to a different time period, which is more accurately described as *The Day of God's Wrath* or *The Day of God's Judgement*. Both are tumultuous times but for different reasons. The Great Tribulation comes from the hatred of men and the natural birth pains of the earth but The Day of Wrath is the time period when the pronouncements of doom written on the scroll are actually read and enacted by God Himself. Once we understand this transition we will gain much more clarity.

Another question worth answering here is, "Why does it matter that we understand this?" Why do we need to know that we will go through the Great Tribulation? Isn't ignorance bliss? Shouldn't we just forget about the future and focus on the here and now? Many people refuse to get into Revelation or get caught up in Tribulation arguments because they don't think it matters at all. However, if it didn't matter, God wouldn't have extended himself to reveal it to us. In John 15, Jesus explains why he warns us of hate and persecution ahead of time: *"I have told you these things so that you won't abandon your faith. For you will be expelled from the synagogues, and the time is coming when those who kill you will think they are doing a holy service for God. This is because they have never known the Father or me. Yes, I'm telling you these things now, so that when they happen, you will remember my warning." (John 16:1-4)*

The reason we need to know that we'll go through the Great Tribulation is so that we won't be abandon our faith when it happens. Jesus wants to take the element of surprise out of the way. You see, if we've been taught that we'll be raptured out of the earth before life gets difficult and then find ourselves being beaten and imprisoned, obviously we're going to be confused. We might start questioning Jesus. *"Is he really there? Is he really God? Is he really in control? He said he would have rescued us by now and he hasn't."* Those are the kinds of thoughts that would go through our minds. Many would lose hope and abandon the faith because it would all seem to be a lie.

However, if Jesus tells us ahead of time that we're going to suffer, it changes our attitude completely. When it happens we'll think, *"yes of course, this is exactly what he said would happen."* We'll brace ourselves and set our faces like flint knowing that everything is proceeding as planned. In a way, the eruption of tribulation will actually bolster our faith because we knew it had to come, we know he is still in control, we know it's bringing us closer to the end and we know that eternal life lies on the other side.

## ATTENTION TURNS BACK TO ISRAEL

Before the seventh and final seal is opened and God's judgement is read aloud, not only is the church taken out of the way, but Jesus pauses for another very important purpose. Revelation describes it like this:

*"Then I saw four angels standing at the four corners of the earth, holding back the four winds so they did not blow on the earth or the sea, or even on any tree. And I saw another angel coming up from the east, carrying the seal of the living God. And he shouted to those four angels, who had been given power to harm land and sea, Wait! Don't harm the land or the sea or the trees until we have placed the seal of God on the foreheads of his servants."* (Rev 7:1-3)

So there's a moment of tremendous calm on earth - calm before the storm you might say - while the servants of God are sealed. Who are these servants? Isn't the church pretty much gone by now? It seems so. And when it left, the "Church Age" or the

"Age of the Gentiles" actually came to an end. Basically, the story is now reverting back to those with whom it began: Israel. The Bible says:

*"And I heard how many were marked with the seal of God - 144,000 were sealed from all the tribes of Israel:*

| | |
|---|---|
| *from Judah* | *12,000* |
| *from Reuben* | *12,000* |
| *from Gad* | *12,000* |
| *from Asher* | *12,000* |
| *from Naphtali* | *12,000* |
| *from Manasseh* | *12,000* |
| *from Simeon* | *12,000* |
| *from Levi* | *12,000* |
| *from Issachar* | *12,000* |
| *from Zebulun* | *12,000* |
| *from Joseph* | *12,000* |
| *from Benjamin* | *12,000"* |

*(Rev 7:4-8)*

So the Gentile church is gone but 144,000 Jewish believers are sealed and left on the earth.

We need to turn to Romans 11 to be reminded that God had always intended to turn his attention back to Israel once the full number of Gentile converts had been saved. This is a shortened version of that chapter containing the key passages:

*"I ask, then, has God rejected his own people, the nation of Israel? Of course not!... No, God has not rejected his own people, whom he chose from the very beginning. Do you realize what the Scriptures say about this? Elijah the prophet complained to*

*God about the people of Israel and said, "LORD, they have killed your prophets and torn down your altars. I am the only one left, and now they are trying to kill me, too." And do you remember God's reply? He said, "No, I have 7,000 others who have never bowed down to Baal!" It is the same today, for a few of the people of Israel have remained faithful because of God's grace— his undeserved kindness in choosing them... So this is the situation: Most of the people of Israel have not found the favour of God they are looking for so earnestly. A few have—the ones God has chosen—but the hearts of the rest were hardened. As the Scriptures say, "God has put them into a deep sleep. To this day he has shut their eyes so they do not see, and closed their ears so they do not hear."... Did God's people stumble and fall beyond recovery? Of course not! They were disobedient, so God made salvation available to the Gentiles. But he wanted his own people to become jealous and claim it for themselves. Now if the Gentiles were enriched because the people of Israel turned down God's offer of salvation, think how much greater a blessing the world will share when they finally accept it.... I want you to understand this mystery, dear brothers and sisters, so that you will not feel proud about yourselves. **Some of the people of Israel have hard hearts, but this will last only until the full number of Gentiles comes to Christ. And so all Israel will be saved.** As the Scriptures say, "The one who rescues will come from Jerusalem, and he will turn Israel away from ungodliness. And this is my covenant with them, that I will take away their sins."*

*Many of the people of Israel are now enemies of the Good News, and this benefits you Gentiles. Yet they are still the people he loves because he chose their ancestors Abraham, Isaac, and Jacob. For God's gifts and his call can never be withdrawn. Once, you Gentiles were rebels against God, but when the people of Israel rebelled against him, God was merciful to you instead. Now they are the rebels, and God's mercy has come to you so that they, too, will share in God's mercy." (Romans 11)*

Basically Paul is saying that most of Israel have had their eyes closed and their hearts hardened to the truth about Jesus Christ and this is punishment for their rejection of him 2000 years ago. During that time, salvation has been offered to the Gentiles instead. From that time until now, we have been living in the "Age of the Gentiles" or "The Church Age". Paul says that this Age will only last until the full number of Gentile converts comes to Christ. And when that Age is over, God will revert his attention back to Israel again. You see, even though it seems like all Israel has gone astray, rejecting Jesus and the Father who sent him, there is actually a small remnant of believers left - just like in Elijah's day.

Remember how Elijah thought Israel was completely devoid of faith and complained that his countrymen had killed God's prophets, but God knew of a 7,000 strong remnant who belonged to him? In the last days, and even now as we approach them, while it appears as though Israel is devoid of true faith and we bemoan the fact that they killed God's anointed Son, once again, God will actually know of a small remnant...and it is indeed small...just 144,000...who belong to him. They may be referred to as Messianic Jews - Jewish believers. There are 12,000 from each of the Jewish tribes and in that sense, "all Israel will be saved." (Rom 11:26) That phrase doesn't literally mean that every single Jewish person will be saved. It simply means that 'all Israel' is composed of twelve tribes and each of those tribes will be represented in this final number. If one of the twelve tribes were lost or cut off, it could not be said that *all* Israel was saved. But the fact is that God knows the lineage of every Jewish person in the world and an equal number from each tribe will be sealed at this time. They will remain on earth throughout the Day of God's Wrath.

In this moment you may notice strong similarities with the Passover in Exodus. In those days, the Israelites were living in captivity in Egypt and God was sending plagues upon their tormentors. As an ultimate act of judgement, God warned his people that he was going to pass through Egypt and strike down all the first born babies in the land. In order to identify themselves as his, the Israelites had to sacrifice a lamb and then smear the blood on their door frame. God said, *"the blood on your doorposts will serve as a sign, marking the houses where you are staying. When I see the blood, I will pass over you. This plague of death will not touch you when I strike the land of Egypt." (Exodus 12:13)* So the Israelites would live through the experience but they wouldn't be harmed by any of it.

It's a similar situation during the Day of Wrath.

God is preparing to pour out his wrath on the whole earth but these 144,000 Israelites who have been sealed with the blood of the Lamb, even though they're in the midst of the judgement, won't be harmed by any of it. God will 'pass over' them again.[10]

Their job during the Day of Wrath is to take over from the church as God's witnesses on the earth. They will preach the Gospel to the four corners of the world.

Now let's read about the opening of the seventh and final seal.

## THE SEVENTH SEAL

*"When the Lamb broke the seventh seal on the scroll, there was silence throughout heaven for about half an hour. I saw the seven angels who stand before God, and they were given seven trumpets." (Rev 8:1-2)*

Just as there is calm before the storm on earth, there is calm before the storm in heaven. As above, so below. There is complete silence in heaven for half an hour. The *"seven angels who stand before God"* are then given trumpets. I believe these seven angels are represented in our image by the seven torches with burning flames:

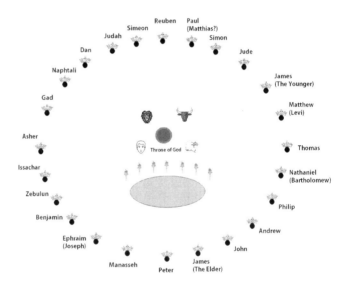

Remember how John had previously written, *"And in front of the throne were seven torches with burning flames. They are the seven spirits of God." (Rev 4:5)* I think it's fair to deduce that these angels - these seven spirits of God - are the ones who have just been given a trumpet each.

Next, another angel, not represented in the illustration, enters the room:

*"Then another angel with a gold incense burner came and stood at the altar. And a great amount of incense was given to him to mix with the prayers of God's people as an offering on the gold altar before the throne. The smoke of the incense, mixed with the prayers of God's holy people, ascended up to God from the altar where the angel had poured them out. Then the angel filled the incense burner with fire from the altar and threw it down upon the earth; and thunder crashed, lightning flashed, and there was a terrible earthquake." (Rev 8:1-5)*

You know all those prayers for justice that you've ever prayed? You know all those times that you've seen the wicked triumph and you've begged for God to do something about it? The times you've been so depressed or furious because evil never seems to lose? All those news reports of animal cruelty or child abuse. All those savage murders. Those demonically inspired tyrants and despots forcing whole nations into misery and war. The subjugation and the slavery. The trafficking. The thefts, the deception and the rapes. The selfishness and the greed. Have you ever ached for justice? Have you ever pleaded with God to take vengeance on the evil ones and to make things right? If you have, the prayers you have prayed are not wasted or forgotten, even though they haven't been answered right away. They're currently being stored up, as is beautifully described in this passage. The prayers of God's people rise up to his throne like the smoke from burning incense and on the Day of Wrath, God will announce that the time has come for them to be answered with thunder, lightning and a terrible earthquake.

What this passage is telling us is that although God is personally offended by sin - even more offended than you and I - and burns with a righteous anger for the wickedness that he has seen, that's only partly what the Day of Wrath is about. He's also furious on *our* behalf. He's heard our prayers, he's seen our tears, he's seen us suffer and he is apocalyptically angry with all those who have hurt, cheated and persecuted his little ones. He will see to it that justice is served.

It reminds us of the passage where Paul says, *"Dear friends, never take revenge. Leave that to the righteous anger of God. For the Scriptures say, "I will take revenge; I will pay them back," says the LORD." (Romans 12:19)*

Very simply, the Day of Wrath is pay back time. Justice *will* be done. Do not doubt it. Maybe not today, maybe not tomorrow, but that day *will* come. If we have full confidence in these words it takes a huge burden off our shoulders. It releases us from grudges and unforgiveness. It means we should never exact revenge or meet hate with hate. Instead, we should love our enemies, forgive freely, bless those who curse and keep offering the gospel of salvation, knowing that those who continually reject it and persecute us are just storing up wrath for themselves. They are heaping burning coals onto their own heads and are to be pitied for hardening their hearts and allowing evil to consume them. There's something incredibly liberating when you realise that God will take care of everything on our behalf. It frees us to love even those who hate us. In the end we will be vindicated. The more faith we have in that the more free we become. And as we will soon see, as bad as the Tribulation was, it will be nothing compared to what God has stored up for the world on the Day of Wrath. *"It is a terrible thing to fall into the hands of the living God."* (Heb 10:31)

This passage also tells us that if you want to do something of truly eternal significance, then pray. Prayers will continue to have power long after you're gone. Indeed, they will continue to have power until the end of time. There are even people who are Christians today because of the prayers of departed parents and grandparents.

So the seven seals have been now broken, the scroll has been opened and the judgements are about to be read. There are seven pronouncements of doom on the earth and each one will be preceded by a trumpet blast from one of the seven angels. And remember, the only people left on the earth throughout this time will be those who have rejected Christ and the 144,000 Jewish believers, who will be shielded from any harm, and whose job it is to witness to them through the Day of Wrath, in the hope that some will repent and be saved.

Here's a chart of the timeline so far:

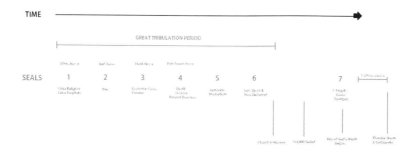

# CHAPTER 4. THE SEVEN TRUMPETS
## (THE DAY OF GOD'S WRATH)

Just as the first four seals (four horsemen) belonged together and the final three were slightly different, the same applies to the trumpets. Let's examine the first four trumpets together now as they're relatively straightforward:

## THE FIRST TRUMPET

*"The first angel blew his trumpet, and hail and fire mixed with blood were thrown down on the earth. One-third of the earth was set on fire, one-third of the trees were burned, and all the green grass was burned." (Rev 8:7)*

The first judgement is hail and fire mixed with blood falling from the sky. What would cause hail and fire mixed with blood to fall from the sky? Some suggest a volcanic eruption. That would certainly explain the image of fire falling from the sky. And there have been previous examples of blood-red coloured rain falling to earth because of dust being thrown into the air and mixing with the water as it falls from the clouds. Others speculate that this is describing a near miss with an asteroid. An interesting theory, and the one that I lean towards, is that solar flares will be to blame. Physicist Professor Michio Kaku recently stated that *"the sun is having a temper tantrum, and it's getting worse and worse."* He continued by saying, *"My greatest fear is the earth getting hit by a large solar flare, and all hell could break loose!"*[1]

Whatever it is, clearly it will have a devastating impact on the planet. One third of the earth's surface is going to be scorched by fire.

## THE SECOND TRUMPET

*"Then the second angel blew his trumpet, and a great mountain of fire was thrown into the sea. One-third of the water in the sea became blood, one-third of all things living in the sea died, and one-third of all the ships on the sea were destroyed." (Rev 8:8-9)*

When the second trumpet is blown, what definitely appears to be a massive volcano, erupts and then falls into the sea. This has a devastating impact on a third of the sea, killing the marine life and destroying the ships in the area. This obvious reference to a volcano at the second trumpet probably eliminates the idea that the first trumpet disaster was also a volcano. That's why I tend to lean towards the idea of solar flares.

## THE THIRD TRUMPET

*"Then the third angel blew his trumpet, and a great star fell from the sky, burning like a torch. It fell on one-third of the rivers and on the springs of water. The name of the star was Bitterness. It made one-third of the water bitter, and many people died from drinking the bitter water." (Rev 8:10-11)*

John describes a star falling from the sky burning like a torch. Stars can often represent angels in Biblical imagery but in this case, his description is almost certainly that of a literal meteorite. When it hits the ground it seems to have some kind of contaminating effect on the fresh water supply and a third of the earth's drinkable water becomes polluted. Many people will die from drinking that water.

## THE FOURTH TRUMPET

*"Then the fourth angel blew his trumpet, and one-third of the sun was struck, and one-third of the moon, and one-third of the stars, and they became dark. And one-third of the day was dark, and also one-third of the night." (Rev 8:12)*

When the fourth trumpet is blown, there are more problems with the sun, moon and stars. Since the sun had already been described as going dark and the moon had already been described as turning blood-red at the sixth seal, we must deduce that those previous events were only temporary solar and "blood-moon" lunar eclipses. Such things are relatively common so the sixth seal eclipses must have been unusual in some way to signify the transition out of the Tribulation and into the Day of Wrath...but no lasting damage will have been done. Here however, it seems that there *is* severe and permanent damage to the sun, moon and a stars, which all lose a third of their brightness.

Not only will this create more darkness on the earth but obviously a diminished sun will lead to a drop in temperatures too. Since earth's temperatures are finely tuned for life to flourish, a drop of a third will cause significant problems in many areas and leave currently habited places uninhabitable.

It's also worth noting that the problems unleashed by the seven seals will still be rampant and increasing in force throughout the seven trumpets. There's no mention of the four horsemen being called back or the broken seals being re-sealed. So all the while there will be an increase in false prophets, famines, economic crises, natural disasters and wars etc.

Our timeline now looks something like this:

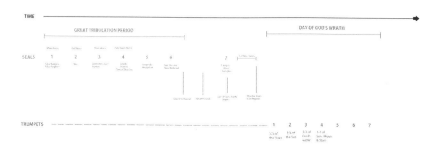

# THE FIFTH TRUMPET (aka THE FIRST TERROR)

The judgements that come with the final three trumpets are slightly different from the first four and they're harder to interpret. They are specifically described as three "woes" or three "terrors" that are going to be inflicted upon the earth. John says:

*"Then I looked, and I heard a single eagle crying loudly as it flew through the air, "Terror, terror, terror to all who belong to this world because of what will happen when the last three angels blow their trumpets.""* (Rev 8:13)

Clearly, the final three judgements are going to step things up a notch. As we explore them, notice that whereas the first four trumpets described problems with the natural world, the final three herald problems which are primarily rooted in the *super*natural world. That's why the Bible will use a lot of metaphorical imagery for these final trumpets - it's often describing unseen things that we have no natural reference points for. Don't be intimidated by the imagery though. It just takes a little patience and exploration to attain the meanings.

The fifth trumpet is described like this:

*"Then the fifth angel blew his trumpet, and I saw a star that had fallen to earth from the sky, and he was given the key to the shaft of the bottomless pit. When he opened it, smoke poured out as though from a huge furnace, and the sunlight and air turned dark from the smoke.*

*Then locusts came from the smoke and descended on the earth, and they were given power to sting like scorpions. They were told not to harm the grass or plants or trees, but only the people who did not have the seal of God on their foreheads. They were told not to kill them but to torture them for five months with pain like the pain of a scorpion sting. In those days people will seek death but will not find it. They will long to die, but death will flee from them!*

*The locusts looked like horses prepared for battle. They had what looked like gold crowns on their heads, and their faces looked like human faces. They had hair like women's hair and teeth like the teeth of a lion. They wore armour made of iron, and their wings roared like an army of chariots rushing into battle. They had tails that stung like scorpions, and for five months they had the power to torment people. Their king is the angel from the bottomless pit; his name in Hebrew is Abaddon, and in Greek, Apollyon—the Destroyer.*

*The first terror is past, but look, two more terrors are coming!"*
*(Rev 9:1-12)*

Iron-clad locusts with hair like women and teeth like lions...see how there is a noticeable step up in the difficulty of the imagery? So let's walk through it carefully.

Firstly, John sees *"a star that had fallen to earth from the sky"* holding a key. What is this "star"? Well, in scripture, stars metaphorically represent angels (see Job 38:7) and since this "star" is called a "he" and is seen to be performing the actions of a personality - namely unlocking the bottomless pit - we can safely assume that this is indeed an angel, rather than a literal star. Some try to pin down his identity in greater detail and suggest this is Satan. Certainly Satan is described as a falling star in other parts of the Bible (see Luke 10:18, Isaiah 14:12) but it's not him. Indeed, towards the end of Revelation we'll see this same angel - the one who holds the keys to the bottomless pit - grabbing Satan to throw him in there. So this is a distinct character. Revelation doesn't name him so his identity is actually not very important. The point is that he opens up the bottomless pit and releases a plague of 'locusts' from within.

That brings us onto the next puzzling part...what are these bizarre sounding locusts actually depicting?

They are described as having the hair of women, the teeth of lions, armour of iron and human-like faces. Clearly these are not literal descriptions of locusts but are metaphorical (and grotesque) pictures of something else. The big clue as to what they are is in the fact that they're released from a place called "the bottomless pit". The bottomless pit is actually identified in several other passages of the Bible as a prison where evil or demonic spirits are currently being detained until the day of judgement.

Jude refers to the pit when he says, *"And I remind you of the angels who did not stay within the limits of authority God gave them but left the place where they belonged. God has kept them securely chained in prisons of darkness, waiting for the great day of judgment."(Jude 1:6)*

Peter talks about this pit, calling it Tartarus, when he says, *"For God did not spare even the angels who sinned. He threw them into Tartarus, in gloomy pits of darkness, where they are being held until the day of judgment."(2 Peter 2:4)*

When Jesus was casting out a group of demons called "Legion" in Galilee, remember how they pleaded with him not to send them to the pit? Luke records it like this: *"As soon as [the demon possessed man] saw Jesus, he shrieked and fell down in front of him. Then he screamed, "Why are you interfering with me, Jesus, Son of the Most High God? Please, I beg you, don't torture me!" For Jesus had already commanded the evil spirit to come out of him. This spirit had often taken control of the man. Even when he was placed under guard and put in chains and shackles, he simply broke them and rushed out into the wilderness, completely under the demon's power.*

*Jesus demanded, "What is your name?"*

*"Legion," he replied, for he was filled with many demons. The demons kept begging Jesus not to send them into the bottomless pit." (Luke 8:28-31)*

The pit is a place of unfathomable depth and darkness. The Greek suggests a kind of shaft or well. And both Peter and Jude seem to allude to the fact that many of the evil spirits who are detained there are being punished for a very specific sin a long time ago. This could refer to some of those who joined Satan's rebellion in heaven before the dawn of time, but perhaps more likely, it could refer to those angels who had sexual relations with women to produce the Nephilim in Genesis (6:4). I believe it's the latter of those explanations. It also explains why those evil spirits are constantly looking for human bodies to inhabit.

Either way, the highest ranking angel currently being detained in the bottomless pit is called Abaddon (or Apollyon), which means "The Destroyer". There's no reason to believe that Abaddon is Satan as some suppose. Indeed, quite the opposite. The Bible makes it clear that Satan does not reside in the pit right now and will not be thrown into it until much later. Therefore, Abaddon, the beast from the pit, appears to be a distinct character. The fact that he is named is also significant. (Remember his name for later.)

Both Jude and Peter specified that the evil spirits in the pit are being held until the day of judgement and here, as the fifth trumpet is blown, that day has arrived. Abaddon leads the hoard of demons out of the unlocked pit and into the world where they are given permission to torture and torment, but not to kill. They will most likely cause this torment by possessing the bodies of the godless, just like "Legion" had done to the man in Galilee. That man had become so mentally troubled that he went insane, running naked into the wilderness and living in a cemetery. These evil spirits who were confined to the pit until this moment will inflict similar torment on people in the last days. They will cause emotional anguish, mental distress, restlessness and severe depression in the people of the world. Sometimes the worst pain is internal. But demons are also very capable of inflicting physical harm too. Indeed, self-harm or cutting often has a demonic root. So severe will the misery and madness be, that people will actually long to die to escape it.

Remember when God allowed Saul to be tormented by an evil spirit in 1 Samuel 16 because of his disobedience? Saul could only find relief when David played his harp. The people in the last days will be similarly tormented but will find no such relief - the Bible says that the torture will last for five whole months (150 days). That's the length of the fifth trumpet. Five months, incidentally, is the same length of time that Noah's flood lasted (Genesis 7:24). "As in the days of Noah" indeed!

## DAY OF GOD'S WRATH

Finally, the Bible makes it clear these evil spirits are allowed to touch *"only the people who did not have the seal of God on their foreheads."* The 144,000 will be spared this calamity. The fact that God can, and does, set such strict boundaries on the activities of the demons reminds us just how much he is in control. Down on earth it will seem like all hell has broken loose but actually, everything is being enacted just as God decreed. It's a bit like the book of Job where God allows Satan to cause suffering for him and his family, but sets very tight limits on how far Satan can go.

God always sets the boundaries. God is always in control.

# THE SIXTH TRUMPET (aka THE SECOND TERROR)

There's so much happening around the sixth and seventh trumpets and so much overlap between the two as God brings the Day of Wrath to completion, that almost all of Revelation from this point onwards will focus on that time period. Indeed, it's interesting that God only devotes about five chapters to all the seven seals and the first five trumpets combined, but then devotes around 10 chapters - double the amount - to the final two trumpets. It's clear that in God's eyes, this is the very centre of end-time prophecy. Everything else has just been leading up to this moment.

With that in mind, let's start with the sixth trumpet.

*"Then the sixth angel blew his trumpet, and I heard a voice speaking from the four horns of the gold altar that stands in the presence of God. And the voice said to the sixth angel who held the trumpet, "Release the four angels who are bound at the great Euphrates River." Then the four angels who had been prepared for this hour and day and month and year were turned loose to kill one-third of all the people on earth. I heard the size of their army, which was 200 million mounted troops." (Rev 9:13-16)*

Here we're told about four angels who have been bound near the Euphrates river but who are turned loose to kill a third of the people on earth. Here's a map to show the region we're talking about:

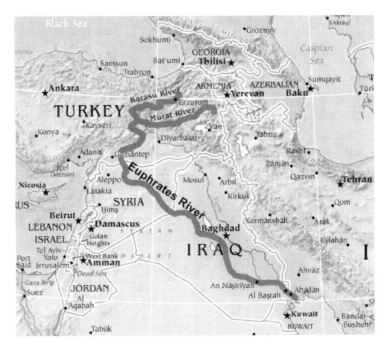

NB: The country on the right of Iraq is Iran. The country to the South of Iraq and Jordan is Saudi Arabia.

We can see from the map that the Euphrates passes through 3 countries - Turkey, Syria and Iraq - and very close to the border of another - Iran. In fact, that border is disputed territory. So there are four countries around the Euphrates and four angels who are bound there. This may not be a coincidence. Indeed, it may suggest that the four angels are the demonic "spirit princes" over those nations.

Remember when Daniel prayed by the Tigris river in Babylon (Iraq) an angel came to him and said, *"Don't be afraid, Daniel. Since the first day you began to pray for understanding and to humble yourself before your God, your request has been heard in heaven. I have come in answer to your prayer. But for twenty-one days the spirit prince of the kingdom of Persia blocked my way. Then Michael, one of the archangels, came to help me, and I left him there with the spirit prince of the kingdom of Persia. Now I am here to explain what will happen to your people in the future, for this vision concerns a time yet to come."(Daniel 10:12-14)*

This passage suggests that Satan has stationed demonic spirit princes over each nation of the world. In Daniel's case, when he started praying, God despatched an angel to see him, but the demonic spirit prince over Persia (Iran) blocked the angel's way and he required backup from the Archangel Michael to push through the blockade. Michael, incidentally, has been stationed over Israel by God. We know this because later in Daniel we read he is, *"Michael, the archangel who stands guard over your nation." (Dan 12:1)* And since the word 'Archangel' can actually be translated as 'the great prince'[2], it seems God has established 'princes' over nations too. Or at least one nation!

The Bible doesn't mention spirit princes - good or evil - over many other nations (only Greece[3]) but if there are - and it's not an unreasonable deduction to make - then the four angels bound at the Euphrates could well be the demonic spirit princes of Turkey, Syria, Iraq and Iran. Since current national boundaries didn't exist when the New Testament was written, we need to be open to the idea that it could include other nearby nations such as Saudia Arabia too. Whoever these four angels are, they are certainly fallen ones. The Bible never describes God's own angels as being "bound" in any way.

The word "bound" is actually an interesting one. It instantly suggests the idea of being tied up or imprisoned, and indeed, the Hebrew root word *"asur" can* mean "fastened" or "tied". However, it can also mean "restricted" or "forbidden". So when John says they are *bound* at the Euphrates, it probably doesn't mean that they are imprisoned there - if they were imprisoned or chained they would have been in the bottomless pit and released during the fifth trumpet. It probably just means that they are currently restricted to operate in that area around the Euphrates. It's a bit like when criminals are under house arrest. They are tagged and restricted from travelling too far from home or from leaving the country. In other words, they have a certain amount of freedom but are bound to a distinct geographical area. These four angels are probably in a similar kind of state. And if they ever do leave their restricted area, they would find themselves in the pit as punishment.

Repeating what Jude said, *"And I remind you of the angels who did not stay within the limits of authority God gave them but left the place where they belonged. God has kept them securely chained in prisons of darkness, waiting for the great day of judgment."(Jude 1:6)*

It seems that any angel who disobeys God by moving outwith the boundaries or authority He has given them are thrown into the pit.

John says that when the sixth trumpet is blown, all restrictions on their freedom will be removed and they'll be turned loose to leave the Euphrates area. Effectively they'll be free to wage war on the whole earth. And unlike the evil spirits from the pit, who were only given authority to torture, these four angels, along with their army, will be given authority *"to kill one-third of all the people on earth."* That army will be 200 million strong. John describes what it looks like:

*"And in my vision, I saw the horses and the riders sitting on them. The riders wore armour that was fiery red and dark blue and yellow. The horses had heads like lions, and fire and smoke and burning sulphur billowed from their mouths. One-third of all the people on earth were killed by these three plagues—by the fire and smoke and burning sulphur that came from the mouths of the horses. Their power was in their mouths and in their tails. For their tails had heads like snakes, with the power to injure people." (Rev 9:13-19)*

Are the 200 million a spiritual demonic army or are we reading about a modern war of some kind? Are the horses with heads like lions and smoke billowing from their mouths vivid pictures of evil spirits, or are they John's attempts to describe modern war machinery with a first century vocabulary? Opinion is divided on this. But since spiritual events dictate physical events, I suggest that it's probably both! An army of 200 million demons could take control of 200 million human beings and cause them to wage war on the earth's inhabitants. We have further evidence to support this theory later in Revelation 16:13 where the Bible makes it clear that demonic spirits will be primarily responsible for gathering the nations of the earth together for the climactic battle of Armageddon. Oftentimes, world leaders make decisions and go to war under the influence of demons without realising it. And that's why we should pray for them.

To put this into context though, the Normandy Landings on D-Day in 1944 - one of the biggest military operations in history up until that point - 'only' involved 156,000 American, British and Canadian troops. In 1991, the 34 nation coalition that liberated Kuwait from Saddam Hussein's Iraq during the Gulf War was comprised of 'just' 1 million troops. So you can see that the world has never been remotely close to witnessing an army of 200 million. Indeed, it's thought that a human army of 200 million would cover an area one mile wide and eighty-five miles deep!

With a population of 1.35 billion, China is currently the only single nation in the world that could muster those kind of numbers. Therefore, many people have tried to pin this event on them. This was particularly true during the 20th Century when Communism was on the rise and any country subscribing to it was believed by the West to be an insidious threat. Today however, in a post-Cold War world, it seems incredibly unlikely that the Chinese would suddenly decide to annihilate a third of the human population. There's no ideological reason for them to do this. They also have no discernable connection to the Euphrates river. The Chinese hypothesis seems to exist purely because of their size and because people tend to view prophecy through the lens of current events. As the Cold War has moved from "current event" to "historical event", so have the chances of this theory making much sense.

And I guess this highlights our problem in identifying the army in general. Revelation is progressive. In other words, it becomes clearer, the closer we get to the events taking place. What looked like the answer to previous generations doesn't look at all like the answer today. And even from this distance, it's incredibly difficult to predict how geopolitical tensions will change in the years ahead. For example, everyone agrees that 9/11 fundamentally changed the world but who could have predicted it? And who could have accurately predicted the precise consequences? The economic collapse in 2008 changed the world too, but who knew it was coming? Likewise, an event could happen tomorrow that will instantly change our view of the sixth trumpet. Suddenly something that seemed hidden or obscure will come clearly into view. What's just as likely to happen is that a lot of small changes will occur in the coming years and as they take place, the sixth trumpet will begin to reveal itself gradually. We should therefore stay watchful to discern what we see.

However it comes about, the event will be easily recognised by those who live through it - primarily because of the enormous death toll. A third of humanity being wiped out will obviously represent the worst single loss of human life in all history. A number that - allowing for population changes and the loss of life from the previous seals and trumpets - will probably be in the region of 1.5 - 2 billion.

Indeed, some have even estimated that when the deaths of the fourth seal are added to the Christian genocide of the fifth seal, and then added to the worldwide slaughter of this sixth trumpet, as much as 50% of the world's population, or more, will have been annihilated by this time. At today's population levels, that would be something in the order of 3.5 billion - the equivalent of the entire populations of China, India, USA, Indonesia, Brazil and Pakistan combined. All gone.

This is going to be simply unmistakeable.

I will put forward one interesting theory about the 200 million before moving on because, as I write, it seems to be by far the most plausible explanation. Since these four angels are bound in the Islamic heartlands of the Middle East, and since the devastation originates there but affects the whole earth, the sixth trumpet may represent an Islamic attack. The Pew Forum reports that Muslims currently make up 1.6 billion of the earth's population (20%) so it's easily conceivable that they could raise an army of 200 million from that.[4] Indeed, only 12.5% of their number would be needed to create such an amount. We also know that they have the motivation to mount such an attack as there are many verses in the Quran and Hadith that tell Muslims to fight the unbelievers unceasingly until the whole earth is subdued under the rule of Islam (see Appendix 2). Perhaps most damningly, Islamic prophecies themselves speak of a day when a Messianic figured called the Mahdi will lead Muslims in a huge victory against "all white Europeans, including Americans."[5] So it's on their agenda to do this very thing. And indeed, historically, Islam has been spread by nothing *but* intimidation and violence.[6]

The only problem with the theory that the sixth trumpet represents an Islamic uprising, is that it's hard to conceive of Islamic nations being able to co-ordinate themselves and raise such an organised military machine capable of such destructive force at this point in human history. They fight with themselves as much as they do with anyone else. However, we know that the Muslim Brotherhood are currently trying to consolidate power in that region in the wake of the "Arab Spring" and that part of that process means clearing out the Middle East of Christians. And if we take the four key Euphrates countries one-by-one, we see that Iraq has been through a revolution, Syria is currently involved in one and Iran has always been openly hostile to the West anyway. It has been intent on obtaining nuclear weapons for some time now. And certainly, the Biblical description of fire, smoke and burning sulphur puts us in mind of a nuclear attack. We can also understand that nuclear devices are becoming smaller, easier to conceal, and can be detonated from within containers as small as suitcases. In other words, the Islamic theory still holds water, even today, if we understand it as a terrorist attack rather than a traditional war.

What about Turkey? They're a relatively moderate, even secular country at the moment. But keep an eye on them and watch for that to change. It will be very interesting if the Muslim Brotherhood instigate a revolution in that nation.

Another point of interest in this passage about the 200 million is that it says of the army, *"Their power was in their mouths and in their tails. For their tails had heads like snakes, with the power to injure people"*. That's interesting when we consider that Isaiah, while talking about an end-time attack on Israel, says, *"the prophet who teaches lies is the tail."(Isaiah 9:15)* He equates tails with false prophets. Revelation says these tails have heads like snakes and since snakes are often representations of Satan, we seem to be talking about demonically inspired prophets raising the army. Certainly, this does no harm to the Islamic hypothesis. Especially when we consider that the ultimate authority in Islamic nations doesn't lie with the political authorities, but rather with the "Ayatollahs" - the religious leaders. The Islamic prophets. This is especially true of Iran where the chief Ayatollah is given the title "Supreme Leader of Iran".

It's also interesting that Jesus, when talking about this same end-time attack on Israel, says, *"I have told you these things so that you won't abandon your faith. For you will be expelled from the synagogues, and the time is coming when those who kill you will think they are doing a holy service for God. This is because they have never known the Father or me. " (John 16:1-3)* Who else but Muslims would kill in the belief they are doing a holy service for God?

We'll pick up on this hypothesis again when we explore the end-time attack on Israel in greater depth - that's what the seventh trumpet largely focuses on. In the meantime, John gives us a general picture of the world at this time saying:

*"But the people who did not die in these plagues still refused to repent of their evil deeds and turn to God. They continued to worship demons and idols made of gold, silver, bronze, stone, and wood—idols that can neither see nor hear nor walk! And they did not repent of their murders or their witchcraft or their sexual immorality or their thefts." (Rev 9:20-21)*

Mankind is unrepentant. They could repent - salvation is still available to them - it's just that they've become so stubborn and hard-hearted that they don't want to. This puts us in mind of Pharaoh when the plagues were coming upon Egypt. No matter how much pain he was in, no matter how much destruction befell Egypt, he kept hardening his heart.

I'm also reminded of the recent incident in Woolwich, London, when Private Lee Rigby was shockingly attacked by two Muslim men and beheaded in the street. In the aftermath of that event I posted a status on Facebook denouncing the murder but pointing out that it was in-keeping with the tenets of Islam. My secular contacts quickly turned the discussion into an attack on Christianity, the Crusades and the Inquisition. Furthermore, many of them unfriended and blocked me for my 'intolerance'. So even in the aftermath of a man being beheaded in the street, the latest in a long line of Muslim terrorist attacks, they continued to harden their hearts and instead somehow blamed God. Therefore, I can quite imagine this happening on a much larger scale. The Muslims striking out at the world, the 144,000 pleading with them to see sense and turn to God, and yet the world stubbornly holding to their belief that somehow true Islam isn't to blame and that the Christian God is worse.

The mention of idols of gold, silver, bronze, stone and wood also bring to mind materialism amongst the people of the world. People will be lovers of money and possessions. Foolishly they will prefer hopeless nothings; perishable idols; to God. Murder will be rampant on the earth too. The law of the jungle will prevail. The word "witchcraft" here may well describe New Ageism and occult practices too. Since the original Greek word is *'farmakeia'*, from which we get our word 'pharmacy', it may also describe drug-taking. Pagan religions believe that taking drugs opens up their minds to new spiritual dimensions so there's a close connection between drugs and the occult. This is a concept that has gained traction in the wider world since the 1960s. Finally, people will also be mired in sexual sin, reduced to following their basest instincts with no moral restraint. They will lie, steal and defraud one another as a matter of course. It will be a society of self.

Rampant secular-humanism and materialism on one hand; rampant false religion on the other. The world is starting to take on those characteristics already.

# 5. A TRANSITION
## (THE SEVEN THUNDERS & THE LITTLE SCROLL)

Next comes an intermission in proceedings and it represents a transition in the focus of the book.

*"Then I saw another mighty angel coming down from heaven, surrounded by a cloud, with a rainbow over his head. His face shone like the sun, and his feet were like pillars of fire. And in his hand was a small scroll that had been opened. He stood with his right foot on the sea and his left foot on the land. And he gave a great shout like the roar of a lion. And when he shouted, the seven thunders answered.*

*When the seven thunders spoke, I was about to write. But I heard a voice from heaven saying, "Keep secret what the seven thunders said, and do not write it down." (Rev 10:1-4)*

This is an unusual passage in the sense that Revelation is meant to reveal and yet John is not allowed to write down, or tell us exactly what the seven thunders said. What was the point of showing John this part of the vision if he was not allowed to relay it? What was the point of John even including this in his report?

Well, if nothing else, this verse tells us again that Revelation is progressive. There are things that are 'sealed up' and that can't be known today. They will become evident nearer the time, certainly. But not today. It would be pointless at this juncture to speculate on what the seven thunders might have said. God clearly doesn't want it to be known yet. Perhaps it's information that He wants to keep secret from the enemy until the day arrives. We can only speculate as to his motives. But really, we don't need to. While it's good to be curious about prophecy generally and we should try to discern the signs of the times, it's useless trying to reveal things that God has deliberately kept hidden. They will become apparent in due course and in His own time. This is also why we shouldn't bother trying to set dates for when Jesus Christ will return. He has already said that it can't be known in advance (Matt 24:36).

I believe this event is included in the timeline because God just wants us to know that *some*thing important will happen here. Something significant will happen around the sixth trumpet. People will know it when they see it. And since God always sends his prophets along ahead of time to reveal to the people what he's about to do, God will probably send a prophet along ahead of the enactment of the seven thunders at the right time. Perhaps he will send *two* prophets. (And we'll expand on that theory later.)

John continues:

*"Then the angel I saw standing on the sea and on the land raised his right hand toward heaven. He swore an oath in the name of the one who lives forever and ever, who created the heavens and everything in them, the earth and everything in it, and the sea and everything in it. He said, "There will be no more delay. When the seventh angel blows his trumpet, God's mysterious plan will be fulfilled. It will happen just as he announced it to his servants the prophets."(Rev 10:5-7)*

Here the angel confirms that there is only one more trumpet to go and when it is blown, all things will be fulfilled. The pouring out of God's wrath on the earth will be complete. The angel's stance with one foot on the sea and one on the land denotes an authority over all the earth.

*"Then the voice from heaven spoke to me again: "Go and take the open scroll from the hand of the angel who is standing on the sea and on the land."*

*So I went to the angel and told him to give me the small scroll. "Yes, take it and eat it," he said. "It will be sweet as honey in your mouth, but it will turn sour in your stomach!" So I took the small scroll from the hand of the angel, and I ate it! It was sweet in my mouth, but when I swallowed it, it turned sour in my stomach.*

*Then I was told, "You must prophesy again about many peoples, nations, languages, and kings."(Rev 10:8-11)*

John may have been denied the opportunity to write down what the thunders had said but instead he's given another message on a small scroll. Some people make the mistake of thinking the words of the seven thunders are written *on* the small scroll, but the two are unconnected. Indeed, while John is told that the words of the seven thunders are to be kept secret (or sealed up), we see that the prophecy on the small scroll is an open one. John says, *"in his hand was a small scroll **that had been opened**."* And John is told, *"Go and take the **open** scroll from the hand of the angel..."* There are no seals. So unlike the seven thunders, this message *isn't* hidden or secret.

What is the significance of this small scroll then? And why is it small? It's small because the focus of Revelation is now zeroing in on Israel, but even more specifically, on Jerusalem. It's a mini judgement for God's Holy city within the larger judgement of the Day of Wrath. Indeed, most of Revelation from now on will be focused there.

Remember how I said that Revelation was like Acts in reverse? Acts starts in Jerusalem and then the focus spreads out to Israel, and then around chapter 9, Israel is left behind completely and the focus expands to the wider Gentile church? Well just as Acts expands, Revelation contracts. Revelation starts with the wider Gentile church, then shifts focus to Israel, and now more specifically, focuses narrowly on Jerusalem again. The centre of end-time prophecy is there. Almost the entire second half of the book of Revelation is devoted to the fate of Jerusalem.

Why should God spend so much time focused on Jerusalem? Because, as Zechariah 2:8 tells us, Jerusalem is God's most precious possession. You'll notice that when the Old Testament prophets speak about the end, they focus on Jerusalem's fate too.

Why does John *eat* this little scroll? You may remember Ezekiel doing the same thing. Just like then, John eating the small scroll is symbolic of the fact that God is giving him another prophecy to declare - it's a bit like the Word is being downloaded into him. He's digesting it and it's becoming a part of him. The words he writes will not be his own.

Why does it taste sweet like honey? Because, as Psalm 119:103 says, the Word of God is *"sweeter than honey."* However, the scroll prophetically contains more pronouncements of judgement, which is why it turns sour in his stomach. It's sweet because it's the righteous Word of God but sour because it spells disaster for the world, but again, far more specifically, for Israel and its beating heart: Jerusalem.

Indeed, this marks the start of a period called Jacob's Trouble.

# CHAPTER 6. JACOB'S TROUBLE

Jeremiah prophesied about this time of trouble for Israel saying, *"In all history there has never been such a time of terror. It will be a time of trouble for my people Jacob (Israel)* [1]*. Yet in the end they will be saved!" (Jeremiah 30:7).*

Jacob's Trouble is also mentioned by Jesus in the Olivet Discourse: *"And when you see Jerusalem surrounded by armies, then you will know that the time of its destruction has arrived. Then those in Judea must flee to the hills. Those in Jerusalem must get out, and those out in the country should not return to the city. For those will be days of God's vengeance, and the prophetic words of the Scriptures will be fulfilled. How terrible it will be for pregnant women and for nursing mothers in those days. For there will be disaster in the land and great anger against this people. They will be killed by the sword or sent away as captives to all the nations of the world. And Jerusalem will be trampled down by the Gentiles until the period of the Gentiles comes to an end."(Luke 21:20-24)*

Why is God specifically pouring out his wrath on Israel? Jerusalem even...His Holy city! Because they still have an unpaid debt. There is still some unfinished business between God and his people. And as Jesus says, "the prophetic words of the Scriptures" must be fulfilled.

What prophetic words are these?

Well, back in Daniel's time (around 535BC), Israel had been invaded and taken captive by the Babylonians - this in itself was punishment for disobedience. While in captivity in Babylon, Daniel was praying for God to forgive his nation and to let them return to their own land. He says, *"I went on praying and confessing my sin and the sin of my people, pleading with the LORD my God for Jerusalem, his holy mountain. As I was praying, Gabriel, whom I had seen in the earlier vision, came swiftly to me at the time of the evening sacrifice. He explained to me, "Daniel, I have come here to give you insight and understanding. The moment you began praying, a command was given. And now I am here to tell you what it was, for you are very precious to God. Listen carefully so that you can understand the meaning of your vision.*

*A period of seventy sets of seven has been decreed for your people and your holy city to finish their rebellion, to put an end to their sin, to atone for their guilt, to bring in everlasting righteousness, to confirm the prophetic vision, and to anoint the Most Holy Place." (Daniel 9:20-24)*

Seventy sets of seven is 490 years. This was the length of sentence that God had decreed for his people to atone for their rebellion and guilt. But this would be broken up into segments. Gabriel continues:

*"Now listen and understand! Seven sets of seven plus sixty-two sets of seven will pass from the time the command is given to rebuild Jerusalem until a ruler—the Anointed One—comes. Jerusalem will be rebuilt with streets and strong defences, despite the perilous times." (Daniel 9:24-25)*

Gabriel says that from the moment the Babylonian king allows them to return from slavery and the command is given to rebuild Jerusalem, there would be "Seven sets of seven plus sixty-two sets of seven." That is 49 years + 434 years = 483 years. After those 483 years had passed, the Anointed One would come. This, of course, is a reference to Jesus Christ, the Messiah.

The calculations are complicated due to the fact that the Jewish calendar is lunar rather than solar and has 360 days in a year rather than 365...and that's not to mention the issue of leap-years! However, we can simplify it a little if we understand that 483 Jewish years represents 173,880 days (Jewish day lengths are at least the same as ours!)

Since the command to rebuild Jerusalem after their Babylonian captivity was given by King Antaxerxes on March 16, 445BC[2], all we have to do is add 173,880 days to that date and we should arrive at the coming of Jesus. Incredibly, 173,880 days after March 16, 445BC is April 6, 32AD - the exact date that Jesus is believed to have made his triumphal entry into Jerusalem. The second chapter of Luke tells us that Jesus started his ministry in the 15th year of the reign of Tiberius...that's 29AD...and we know Jesus ministered for three years until the 4th Passover. That brings us to the Passover of 32AD. The prophecy was fulfilled down to the day. The Anointed One arrived right on cue.

However, Israel didn't recognise their Messiah at this point and rejected him. So it was at this exact moment that Israel had their eyes blinded and their hearts hardened so that all things might be fulfilled according to God's plan (he had to be crucified for the sins of the world). Therefore, it was at this same exact moment when Christ was offered to the Gentiles instead and the Church Age began. In other words, after 483 years, the clock stopped ticking on Israel's 490 year sentence. There was a break in the countdown while God's primary relationship switched from Israel to the church. That means there is still one set of seven years left where God has to turn his attention back to Israel so that all prophecy can be fulfilled and the fullness of their sentence can be completed. They still have a seven year debt to pay. And that seven year time period will begin from the moment the Church Age ends.

When did the Church Age end? We noted that the Church Age ended back around the sixth or seventh seal. That's when the church seems to fade away and God returns his attention to Israel, signified by the sealing of the 144,000. This final seven year period that wraps up human history is sometimes called "Daniel's 70th Week". The angel Gabriel continues:

*"After this period of sixty-two sets of seven, the Anointed One will be killed, appearing to have accomplished nothing, and a ruler will arise whose armies will destroy the city and the Temple. The end will come with a flood, and war and its miseries are decreed from that time to the very end. The ruler will make a treaty with the people for a period of one set of seven, but after half this time, he will put an end to the sacrifices and offerings. And as a climax to all his terrible deeds, he will set up a sacrilegious object that causes desecration, until the fate decreed for this defiler is finally poured out on him." (Daniel 9:26-27)*

Gabriel says the Anointed One, Jesus, would die, appearing to have accomplished nothing. At least in their eyes. You see, Israel expected their Messiah to come as a conquering warrior who would establish the nation, crush their enemies and rule the world. Clearly, they didn't expect a suffering Messiah who would be flogged, crucified and buried in a borrowed tomb. They didn't expect that Jerusalem and the temple would be destroyed soon after. Yet, if they paid attention to this prophecy in Daniel, they would have known that this had to happen. And indeed, right on cue, the Roman Emperor Titus sent armies to destroy the Temple in 70AD.

This prophecy also tells us that when the final set of seven years of judgement for Israel begins at the end of time, it will involve a great war, a flood and another ruler, who will initially make a peace treaty with Israel for the seven year stretch, but who will break it half way through. After 3.5 years, 42 months or 1,260 days, he will set up a sacrilegious idol. This idol is sometimes known as the Abomination of Desolation and it will be established on Temple Mount in Jerusalem. The ruler, who we can identify as the Antichrist, will have the authority to do whatever he likes for the second half of the seven year period. And what he likes, unfortunately, is to wage war on the people of Israel. Hence, the term, Jacob's Trouble.

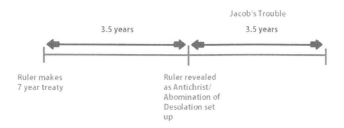

Now let's add that concept to the overall timeline (for clarity, the seven seals are out of picture to the left):

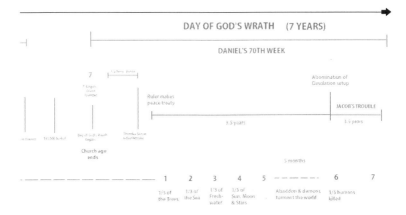

So although Jacob's Trouble will last for 3.5 years from around the sixth trumpet, the Antichrist will actually have been on the scene for at least 3.5 years prior. And although we can only guess as to when his rise to prominence will be, it would make sense if the peace treaty with Israel was signed around the time that the Church Age ends, back around the sixth or seventh seal. This will be when God's primary relationship switches away from the church back to Israel and would set Daniel's 70th Week in motion. He won't be revealed as the Antichrist at that early stage; he will be considered a man of peace. Indeed, people will laud him for his ability to finally bring some stability to that region. Remember Paul wrote, *"When people are saying, "Everything is peaceful and secure," then disaster will fall on them as suddenly as a pregnant woman's labour pains begin. And there will be no escape." (1 Thess 5:3)* Israel will have been lulled into a false sense of security at the time of the attack. The Antichrist's true nature will only be revealed halfway into the seven year peace treaty when he will turn violent. That pivotal moment seems to coincide with the 200 million strong army killing a third of the world. Having orchestrated that, he will then surround Jerusalem looking to invade it and take control. And indeed, he will be allowed to trample on the city for another 3.5 years.

There are hints of Islam in this scenario again. Muhammad began as a man of peace while living in Mecca but then infamously turned into a bloodthirsty warlord after moving to Medina. This may not be a coincidental parallel. Also, Muslim's use the word "hudna" for peace treaties and in reality hudnas are not worth the paper they're written on, believing as they do that they can be legitimately broken at any moment and that they can be used to deceive the enemy by lulling them into a false sense of security. The Antichrist's peace treaty bears the hallmarks of a hudna.

Above all though, it's important to remember that God is allowing this to happen. Although it will seem like the Antichrist is in control as he runs amok over Israel and tears up Jerusalem, ultimately God is still omnipotent. He's merely allowing it to happen so that Israel's sentence can be completed and their guilt atoned for. He has done this in the past by letting surrounding nations invade to take his people captive for a time.

## THE TEMPLE

"Then I was given a measuring stick, and I was told, "Go and measure the Temple of God and the altar, and count the number of worshipers. But do not measure the outer courtyard, for it has been turned over to the nations. They will trample the holy city for 42 months. And I will give power to my two witnesses, and they will be clothed in burlap and will prophesy during those 1,260 days." (Rev 11:1-3)

Before we look at the identity of the two witnesses there are some important pieces of information from this passage to consider.

Firstly, you'll notice the Bible expresses the time of Jacob's Trouble in many different ways. In this passage it says that *"They will trample the holy city for 42 months"* and then in the next sentence it's expressed as *"1,260 days."* It all refers to the same time period. 3.5 years is 42 months, which is 1,260 days. There's a fourth way which is found in Daniel:

*"Then I, Daniel, looked and saw two others [angels] standing on opposite banks of the river. One of them asked the man dressed in linen, who was now standing above the river, "How long will it be until these shocking events are over?"*

*The man dressed in linen, who was standing above the river, raised both his hands toward heaven and took a solemn oath by the One who lives forever, saying, "It will go on for a time, times, and half a time. When the shattering of the holy people has finally come to an end, all these things will have happened.""* (Daniel 12:5-7)

"A time" is one year, "times" is 2 years, and "half a time" is half a year. So *"A time, times, and a half a time"* equals 3.5 years. Which is 42 months or 1,260 days. It's always the same period. Whenever you see these numbers, it's always referring to Jacob's Trouble.

Secondly, notice that John is given a measuring stick and told to *"Go and measure the Temple of God..."* This is significant because it means the Temple of God will exist in Jerusalem during the sixth trumpet. Why is this significant? Because right now the Temple does *not* exist. Indeed, there hasn't been a Temple in Jerusalem since the last one was destroyed by the Romans in 70AD. Where the Temple used to stand on Temple Mount (Mount Moriah), there is now only the Islamic al-Aqsa Mosque and the Dome of the Rock shrine. So obviously, at some point in the future, prior to the sixth trumpet, that Mosque is going to be torn down and a Temple built in its place.

What kind of political situation is going to have to occur before the al-Aqsa mosque is destroyed and replaced with a Jewish Temple? Perhaps the kind of situation where an Antichrist pretends to be on the side of Israel by offering them, as a token of peace, the opportunity to retake control of Temple Mount so that they can build their Temple - only to turn on them once it has been completed so he can use it as an idolatrous throne for himself? We don't know. It's one of those events that doesn't seem to be in view right now but could easily come into view at any time. It could happen tomorrow. We just know that there will be a temple there by the sixth trumpet.

However it happens, when it happens, it will be the third Temple to occupy the site. The first Temple was built by King Solomon and it was destroyed in 586BC when Israel was invaded and taken into slavery in Babylon. The second temple was built when the Israelites returned from that captivity, having been let go by King Antaxerxes. That was the one that Gabriel told Daniel about, the one whose destruction was predicted by Jesus at the beginning of the Olivet Discourse (Matt 24:1-2), and the one that actually was destroyed by the Romans in 70AD. The third temple will be constructed according to the detailed measurements prophesied in Ezekiel 40-44. No temple has yet been built according to Ezekiel's design in those chapters, so it must be a reference to the third one which will occupy Temple Mount in the end-times. We won't go into the specifications here but I recommend that you turn to Ezekiel 40-44 now and examine the measurements.

Is there any evidence that this Temple could be built in the near future? Absolutely. In fact, the importance of a third Temple to the Jews, particularly Orthodox Jews, can't be understated. They believe the building of the third Temple to be absolutely vital for the coming of their Messiah (they didn't recognise him the first time) and are driven to make sure that they gain control of Temple Mount again to herald his arrival. In their eyes, the building of a third Temple wouldn't just anticipate his coming; it would speed it up.

So the third Temple is not, and will not, be driven by Christians. Christians understand that Christ obsoleted the need for a physical Temple. Rather, the whole endeavour is, and will continue to be, driven by Jews - especially Orthodox Jews - who want to have the Temple in its place so they can reinstate daily sacrifices. Again, Christians know that the Mosaic Law that required daily sacrifices has been abrogated by the new covenant, but Orthodox Jews, believing the Mosaic Law to still be applicable, would continue the practice of animal sacrifice to atone for sins if they had the Temple in place. There is no question of them building a Temple and reinstating sacrifices anywhere else either - they would not feel at liberty to move the Holy of Holies to any other location. It must be Temple Mount, Jerusalem.

So strong is the desire to build a third Temple there that most of the plans for its construction are already in place. Indeed, organisations like the Temple Institute and Temple Mount Faithful, have not only produced the building plans according to

Ezekiel's specifications, but they've also made the ritual objects and garments that would be used by the priests within. Some of these objects are on display in the old city right now. The desperate hope of these organisations is that when conditions allow it to be built, everything will be ready ahead of time and the building process will be extremely quick. In fact, so advanced are these plans that it's estimated the whole Temple could be built in as little as 18 months.

As I said, we don't know when the go-ahead will be given - it's one of those events that could happen any day now - but certainly it's plausible that the Antichrist could be the one to negotiate its construction at the outset of the initial 3.5 year period of peace. That would certainly gain the trust of the Jewish people and cause them to drop their guard. Either way, this is a key event that we should be watchful for. When we see control of Temple Mount transferring to the Jews and when we see construction begin on a third Temple, we'll know that another vital piece of the puzzle is falling into place.

## THE TWO WITNESSES

And now we can turn our attention to these enigmatic individuals called "the two witnesses." When Jacob's Trouble begins, God will send these two into the midst of the carnage. They will preach the truth and announce the coming of the Lord. God says, *"And I will give power to my two witnesses, and they will be clothed in burlap and will prophesy during those 1,260 days." (Rev 11:3)*

I mentioned before in relation to the seven thunders that God always sends prophets ahead of time to warn the people of what he is about to do. I believe these two witnesses will therefore be the ones to reveal what the seven thunders said. It's just too coincidental that there is still some hidden information to be revealed around the sixth trumpet and then, right on cue, we read of two witnesses striding onto the scene to prophesy to Jerusalem. And not only will they prophesy, but they will have power to back up their preaching with incredible miracles too:

*"These two prophets are the two olive trees and the two lampstands that stand before the Lord of all the earth. If anyone tries to harm them, fire flashes from their mouths and consumes their enemies. This is how anyone who tries to harm them must die. They have power to shut the sky so that no rain will fall for as long as they prophesy. And they have the power to turn the rivers and oceans into blood, and to strike the earth with every kind of plague as often as they wish." (Rev 11:4-6)*

The two witnesses, although based in Jerusalem - the epicentre of the turmoil - will be spared any harm for the full 1,260 days. Indeed, anyone who tries to harm them will die. I was asked by a friend recently whether I believed that fire would literally come out of their mouths to consume their enemies. I have to say that I don't know whether it's a literal description. Using the KIS approach which I promised to use, that's what the Bible appears to suggest! But I understand the hesitancy. It just seems so... unlikely. Perhaps they will just be able to kill attackers with a spoken word from their mouths and the fire is a metaphor for this effect. It could be that. I don't want lack of faith to be a barrier though so all I will say is that I believe God could give those powers to his prophets if he wanted. Whatever decision you come to, the most important thing here is that these two witnesses will be untouchable as they live under divine protection.

Now the big question is...who are they? Who are these two defiant men strolling around the great city proclaiming the word of God during its darkest hour? Some believe they are Moses and Elijah because, like these two prophets, Moses was known to turn rivers and oceans to blood (Exodus 7) and struck Egypt with many kinds of plagues (Exodus 7-11), while Elijah was known to destroy people with fire (2 Kings 1) and stop the rain (1 Kings 17). In other words, the signs that Moses and Elijah carried out in days gone by match up exactly with those described here. Furthermore, Moses and Elijah significantly appeared beside Jesus at the transfiguration (Matt 17:3-4).

Others claim that these two witnesses are Enoch and Elijah. The main force of this argument lies in the fact that these are the only two people in history never to have tasted death. Since Hebrews 9:27 says, *"each person is destined to die once and after that comes judgment"* there's an argument that they will both have to come back to experience death once before judgement. I think, however, that this is the weakest theory.

A third group of people claim, and I'm one of them, that since Moses, Elijah and Enoch were just ordinary people (it was the power of God that was extraordinary in their lives), God is more than capable of displaying the same power through ordinary people in the end-times too. As such, there is no reason why these two witnesses need to be famous re-incarnations at all. They could just be a 'type' of a prophet who has gone before in the same way that John the Baptist was a type of Elijah. Indeed, remember at the transfiguration, the disciples asked Jesus when Elijah was going to show up in the flesh and Jesus said, *"Elijah has already come, but he wasn't recognised...Then the disciples realized he was talking about John the Baptist. " (Matt 17:12-13)* We, perhaps, should not make the same mistake as the disciples and expect a literal appearance from Elijah, Moses or Enoch, but should rather understand that two will come along who will be *like* them. They will have the same kind of ministry.

I personally believe they will be a type of Moses and a type of Elijah, not only because the miracles they perform so clearly parallel those performed by Moses and Elijah, but because the end-times will parallel the times in which those prophets lived. It will parallel the time of the Exodus when Moses was prominent, in the sense that God is visiting plagues on the land while passing over those who are sealed in blood. (There will also be an exodus occurring as the 144,000 flee from Jerusalem to the wilderness. More about that later.) It will also parallel the time of Elijah in the sense that there will be so little faith in the land. In Elijah's time there were only 7,000 that hadn't bowed the knee to Baal and in the end-times, there were be a similarly small proportion. Similar times will require similar men.

Many people have noted that their description as *"two olive trees and the two lampstands that stand before the Lord of all the earth"* is very reminiscent of Zechariah 4, where two olive trees and *one* lampstand are identified as Joshua and Zerubaabel. But again, even if this connection is worth making, I wouldn't expect Joshua or Zerubabbel to make a literal re-appearance during the end-times. The end-times witnesses will just be a *type* of two prophets who have gone before.

And again, I believe that whoever they are, they will be instantly recognisable when they arrive on the scene in the midst of this terrible time for Israel. Not only because they will be extremely visible, not only because they will come along during the time of Jacob's Trouble, not only because they will be performing miracles, not only because they will be found in Jerusalem and not only because they will be proclaiming the word of the Lord, but because they will be standing in defiance of the Antichrist.

*"When they complete their testimony, the beast that comes up out of the bottomless pit will declare war against them, and he will conquer them and kill them. And their bodies will lie in the main street of Jerusalem, the city that is figuratively called "Sodom" and "Egypt," the city where their Lord was crucified. And for three and a half days, all peoples, tribes, languages, and nations will stare at their bodies. No one will be allowed to bury them. All the people who belong to this world will gloat over them and give presents to each other to celebrate the death of the two prophets who had tormented them." (Rev 11:7-10)*

At the end of the 42 months/1260 days/3.5 years, the beast that came out of the bottomless pit will overcome these two witnesses and kill them. Now there was only one beast who came out of the bottomless pit who was named and that was Abaddon - The Destroyer. None of the other demons were named except him. Therefore, I think we can deduce that he is the one responsible for the deaths of the two witnesses. He will cut them down at God's set time. And we'll talk about how later.

In the meantime, note that Jerusalem is generally so overrun by evil men and in such moral decay that it could figuratively be called "Sodom". Sodom is often held up as the benchmark of depravity in the Bible. Also note that the Israelites are so badly subjugated that it resembles the days of slavery in Egypt. Who would ever have thought of calling Jerusalem "Sodom" or "Egypt"? Names that seem antithetical to everything Jerusalem has traditionally stood for. It's quite a shocking statement to make. Yet those comparisons are not accidental.

Because the two witnesses have been speaking against the immorality and preaching the imminent return of the Lord for three and a half years, this has tormented the consciences of the listeners. And rather than turning to God, they have hardened themselves instead. Proclamation of the truth tends to have that effect. It polarises. There's evidence that some will turn to God at this time but in general, the vast majority will go in the other direction and hate the two witnesses for the words they speak. Therefore, when the two witnesses are finally killed, there will be a time of great rejoicing in Jerusalem. The people will stare and gloat over the bodies which lie in the street for a full three and a half days. In fact, so happy will the non-believers be that they will celebrate the event with a public holiday. Amidst a carnival type atmosphere, people will be exchanging gifts to commemorate the occasion.

*"But after three and a half days, God breathed life into them, and they stood up! Terror struck all who were staring at them. Then a loud voice from heaven called to the two prophets, "Come up here!" And they rose to heaven in a cloud as their enemies watched.*

*At the same time there was a terrible earthquake that destroyed a tenth of the city. Seven thousand people died in that earthquake, and everyone else was terrified and gave glory to the God of heaven.*

*"The second terror is past, but look, the third terror is coming quickly." (Rev 11:3-14)*

So after three and a half days of gloating and celebration, the two witnesses will be resurrected and ascend to heaven in full view of their enemies. At that time another earthquake will strike the city, causing much destruction and the deaths of 7,000 people. Those who don't die and who see the two witnesses being resurrected at the end of Jacob's Trouble, will turn to God for forgiveness. I will later refer to them as 11th hour converts. Because this all happens at the end of the end.

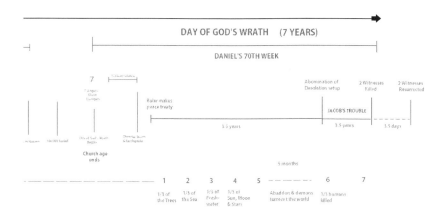

# CHAPTER 7.   THE SEVENTH TRUMPET
## (THE THIRD TERROR)

The seventh trumpet overlaps with the sixth in that it also deals with the 1,260 days of Jacob's Trouble. It will also ultimately bring us into the days immediately *after* Jacob's Trouble ends, culminating with the completion of God's Wrath and the second coming of Christ.

The seventh trumpet represents the third and final 'terror'. As one of the angels had said, *"There will be no more delay. When the seventh angel blows his trumpet, God's mysterious plan will be fulfilled. It will happen just as he announced it to his servants, the prophets."* (Rev 10:7)

The seventh trumpet starts with worship in heaven:

*"Then the seventh angel blew his trumpet, and there were loud voices shouting in heaven:*

*"The world has now become the Kingdom of our Lord and of his Christ,*
  *and he will reign forever and ever."*

*The twenty-four elders sitting on their thrones before God fell with their faces to the ground and worshiped him. And they said,*

*"We give thanks to you, Lord God, the Almighty,*
  *the one who is and who always was,*
*for now you have assumed your great power*
  *and have begun to reign.*

*The nations were filled with wrath,*
   *but now the time of your wrath has come.*
*It is time to judge the dead*
   *and reward your servants the prophets,*
   *as well as your holy people,*
*and all who fear your name,*
   *from the least to the greatest.*
*It is time to destroy*
   *all who have caused destruction on the earth."*

*Then, in heaven, the Temple of God was opened and the Ark of his covenant could be seen inside the Temple. Lightning flashed, thunder crashed and roared, and there was an earthquake and a terrible hailstorm." (Rev 11:15-19)*

The people in heaven recognise that they are about to witness the climax of world history. God's judgement on the earth will come to completion. The worship is quickly followed by a thunderstorm, earthquake and terrible hailstorm.

Next, we see something that has puzzled many but which should be reasonably straightforward for us now that we have our context (Jacob's Trouble) in place.

## THE WOMAN AND THE CHILD

*"Then I witnessed in heaven an event of great significance. I saw a woman clothed with the sun, with the moon beneath her feet, and a crown of twelve stars on her head. She was pregnant, and she cried out because of her labour pains and the agony of giving birth." (Rev 12:1-2)*

Who is this woman? A metaphorical picture of a woman would instantly suggest the church were it not for the fact that the church has gone by now and more importantly, were it not for the fact that the Bible itself provides the translation.

In Genesis 37:9, Joseph had a dream *"and again he told his brothers about it. "Listen, I have had another dream," he said. "The sun, moon, and eleven stars bowed low before me!"* If you read the full story of Joseph, Jacob's son, you'll discover that each of the eleven stars represents one of his brothers. They would each bow before him when he became Prime Minister of Egypt. And each one of those brothers would then go on to become the father of a tribe of Israel (Jacob) - the twelfth of course is Joseph himself. Therefore, this woman is not a personification of the church; it's a personification of God's other covenant people - Israel.

I would narrow it down a little further and say this is a personification of *believing* Israel. I would suggest this is the 144,000 (composed of 12,000 from each tribe) plus, perhaps, those who have responded to their evangelism and accepted Jesus as their Lord and Saviour during the trumpets.

Israel is giving birth to something here but is in tremendous distress as she goes through the birth pains. Remember how often the metaphor of birth-pains was used before? Jesus had said in the Olivet Discourse that the Great Tribulation was just the beginning of the birth pains (Matt 24:8). Jeremiah had prophesied about this time of trouble saying: *"I hear cries of fear; there is terror and no peace. Now let me ask you a question: Do men give birth to babies? Then why do they stand there, ashen-faced, hands pressed against their sides like a woman in labour? In all history there has never been such a time* of terror. It will be a time of trouble for my people Israel. Yet in the end they will be saved!" (Jeremiah 30:4-7) Paul had spoken about the birth pains of the end times too (1 Thessalonians 5:3). It seems that this is the birth that all those birth pains were all leading up to. And whatever is being birthed, Satan clearly doesn't like it:

"Then I witnessed in heaven another significant event. I saw a large red dragon with seven heads and ten horns, with seven crowns on his heads. His tail swept away one-third of the stars in the sky, and he threw them to the earth. He stood in front of the woman as she was about to give birth, ready to devour her baby as soon as it was born." (Rev 12:3-4)

The dragon here is Satan. And indeed, this is the first mention of him in Revelation. When it says that he swept away one-third of the stars in the sky and threw them to earth, that's a reference to the fact that he caused one third of the angels in heaven to fall (i.e. rebel) with him. Satan stands ready to devour this baby as soon as it's born.

"She gave birth to a son who was to rule all nations with an iron rod. And her child was snatched away from the dragon and was caught up to God and to his throne. And the woman fled into the wilderness, where God had prepared a place to care for her for 1,260 days." (Rev 12:5-6)

Who is the son Israel is giving birth to? Well, the main clue is that he is the "son who was to rule all nations with an iron rod." (Rev 12:5) This instantly puts us in mind of Jesus. Jesus is the one who will rule the nations with an iron rod after his second coming. In Revelation 19:15 it says, "From his mouth came a sharp sword to strike down the nations. He will rule them with an iron rod." However, Jesus also tells us that those who overcome the devil will rule alongside him. He says, *"To all who are victorious, who obey me to the very end, To them I will give authority over all the nations. They will rule the nations with an iron rod and smash them like clay pots." (Rev 2:26-27)* So Jesus will rule, but the believers will too! The groom and bride will reign together. The birth metaphor appears to represent Jesus' triumphant second coming with his bride. He will return to Israel and we along with him. That's what is being birthed here. And that's what the birth pains are leading up to.

Before we continue, we have to clear up a common misconception, particularly one that is perpetuated by the Catholic church: the woman here does *not* represent Mary. The Catholic church grasps at the idea that Mary is making a reappearance here in a bid to justify their inordinate obsession with a person who is otherwise only mentioned a handful of times in the New Testament, and not mentioned at all after the first chapter of Acts. Many claim that this passage refers to Mary giving birth to Christ in Bethlehem. Therefore, Catholic art often portrays Mary as having a circle of twelve stars above her head and the moon beneath her feet. Not only does this align her still further with the old pagan goddesses from which the Mary cult sprung, but the whole theory makes no contextual sense.

Why would Revelation suddenly stop its chronological sequence of end-time prophecy and return thousands of years to tell the historical nativity story? There would be no reason to bounce back to an event that's already happened without any kind of warning within the text. The child doesn't fit with Jesus' first coming either. Revelation says that the child is snatched up to

God's throne straight away but we know that Jesus lived on the earth for around 33 years. Also, if it's Jesus' first coming, why is there no reference to his ministry, death or resurrection? For these reasons, we can rule out the idea that it's a reference to the nativity.

What's being described here is an event which is happening chronologically, around the time of the (sixth and) seventh trumpet and more specifically, during the key 1,260 days. This is Jacob's Trouble told from a heavenly perspective. Hence the use of vivid imagery. On earth it seems like abject turmoil but these are actually the birth pains that must be endured for the reappearance of the Saviour and the start of his Millennial reign. Although painful, it's actually leading to something really good.

Revelation confirms that during this time when the Antichrist arrives and his armies surround Jerusalem, Israel will flee from the city to the wilderness. *"And the woman fled into the wilderness, where God had prepared a place to care for her for 1,260 days."* The only people that we are specifically told will escape harm during the Day of Wrath are the 144,000 so I would suggest the woman primarily represents them. But Jesus actually warned all Israel to flee during this time saying, *"those in Judea must flee to the hills. A person out on the deck of a roof must not go down into the house to pack. A person out in the field must not return even to get a coat. How terrible it will be for pregnant women and for nursing mothers in those days. And pray that your flight will not be in winter or on the Sabbath. For there will be greater anguish than at any time since the world began. And it will never be so great again. In fact, unless that time of calamity is shortened, not a single person will survive.*

*But it will be shortened for the sake of God's chosen ones."*
*(Matt 24:16-22)*

It seems that the physically fit will be at an advantage when it comes to evacuating Jerusalem. Luke records Jesus as saying, *"Keep alert at all times. And pray that you might be strong enough to escape these coming horrors and stand before the Son of Man."* *(Luke 21:36)*

The ones who make it to the wilderness will actually be safe for the 1,260 days of Jacob's Trouble. Those who don't will be in for a very hard time. And if it lasted for any longer than the 1,260 days there wouldn't be anyone left. God cuts the time short for the sake of his people. Interestingly, our prayers can affect the time of year this happens. We can make it slightly easier on the believers in those days by praying that it happens in Spring or Summer, rather than Winter. Through this passage we again see that our prayers can have eternal significance.

It's good to get this spiritual, heavenly view on Jacob's Trouble. It gives us much more insight into the interplay between heaven and earth. Including the events that cause the Antichrist to suddenly turn on Israel halfway into his reign:

*"Then there was war in heaven. Michael and his angels fought against the dragon and his angels. And the dragon lost the battle, and he and his angels were forced out of heaven. This great dragon—the ancient serpent called the devil, or Satan, the one deceiving the whole world—was thrown down to the earth with all his angels.*

*Then I heard a loud voice shouting across the heavens,*

"It has come at last—
  salvation and power
and the Kingdom of our God,
  and the authority of his Christ.
For the accuser of our brothers and sisters
  has been thrown down to earth—
the one who accuses them
  before our God day and night.
And they have defeated him by the blood of the Lamb
  and by their testimony.
And they did not love their lives so much
  that they were afraid to die.
Therefore, rejoice, O heavens!
  And you who live in the heavens, rejoice!
But terror will come on the earth and the sea,
  for the devil has come down to you in great anger,
  knowing that he has little time."

When the dragon realized that he had been thrown down to the earth, he pursued the woman who had given birth to the male child. But she was given two wings like those of a great eagle so she could fly to the place prepared for her in the wilderness. There she would be cared for and protected from the dragon for a time, times, and half a time.

Then the dragon tried to drown the woman with a flood of water that flowed from his mouth. But the earth helped her by opening its mouth and swallowing the river that gushed out from the mouth of the dragon. And the dragon was angry at the woman and declared war against the rest of her children—all who keep God's commandments and maintain their testimony for Jesus.

*Then the dragon took his stand on the shore beside the sea."*
*(Rev 12:1-18)*

Around this climactic time of Jacob's Trouble on earth, there's actually a climactic war taking place in heaven too. That might come as a shock to those who are used to thinking of heaven as a serene place, totally devoid of evil.

Indeed, while none of us have seen heaven and it's difficult for us to picture it, I suspect that if we had to try, we would find our imaginations tainted by the pop culture image: a floaty, dreamy, white, colourless, quiet place where loved ones sit on clouds with a ghost of a smile around their faces, in a kind of serene vegetative state, playing harps and staring into the middle distance for all eternity. This cartoonish picture couldn't be further from the truth. Right now, it's a place of tumult and sometimes even war. An equally cartoonish view would be that Satan - all red pyjamas, horns and trident - is currently sitting on a throne in hell, surrounded by flames and despatching his minions to the earth to do his bidding. Satan is, in fact, not only free to roam the earth today (1 Peter 5:8), but he still has access to heaven. The Bible even tells us that he is *"the one who accuses them (the believers) before our God day and night."* In other words, Satan has access to the throne room of God. There is further evidence of this in Job, where Satan is described as entering the throne room of God to accuse Job in person. Satan's continued access to heaven guarantees that it remains a place of tumult.

"As above, so below" is a reliable saying. When there's tumult in heaven, there's tumult on earth. Here we see Satan launching a desperate, all-out war against God for control of heaven. The war, however, is unevenly matched. For a start, Satan has a much smaller army. Only a third of the angels joined him in his rebellion; two thirds stayed loyal to God. Secondly, Satan's doom was set in stone since the day Jesus Christ rose from the grave.

The Archangel Michael leads an army of angels to repel this attack and Satan is defeated. The importance of Michael's role at that time was also emphasised to Daniel: *"At that time Michael, the archangel who stands guard over your nation, will arise. Then there will be a time of anguish greater than any since nations first came into existence. But at that time every one of your people whose name is written in the book will be rescued." (Daniel 12:1)*

The believers on earth seem to play a role in the victory too. It is said that they help defeat Satan *"by the blood of the Lamb and by their testimony."* So clearly the believers on earth are making an impact with prayers, intercession and faithfulness in the face of persecution. In other words, believing Israel are helping with the "re-birthing" of Jesus back into the world through spiritual warfare. It's an interesting insight into the interplay between heaven and earth.

After losing the war for heaven, Satan is thrown out for good. Heaven rejoices at his failure but there is a warning for the earth that since Satan has come down to them, there will be great terror during the final 1,260 day period. Sure enough, Satan lands on earth with a bump, pride bruised and completely enraged because he knows his time is now running out fast. This occurs midway through the Antichrist's peace treaty and that's why he takes control of the Antichrist at that time and goes into all-out war against Israel. His arrival on earth finds him in a state of desperation.

Generally Satan will operate through deceit, sleight of hand and subterfuge. He won't reveal his presence if at all possible. And if he does, he will always appear as an angel of light. It's only in this panicked condition as he realises his impending doom that the mask slips completely and all pretence of goodness is cast aside.

*"When the dragon realized that he had been thrown down to the earth, he pursued the woman who had given birth to the male child. But she was given two wings like those of a great eagle so she could fly to the place prepared for her in the wilderness. There she would be cared for and protected from the dragon for a time, times, and half a time."*

As we've already noted, the 144,000 believers escape to the wilderness and are kept safe there for the full duration of Jacob's Trouble. But one of the ways that Satan will try to get them is through a flood.

*"Then the dragon tried to drown the woman with a flood of water that flowed from his mouth. But the earth helped her by opening its mouth and swallowing the river that gushed out from the mouth of the dragon. And the dragon was angry at the woman and declared war against the rest of her children—all who keep God's commandments and maintain their testimony for Jesus."*

Remember what Daniel said? *"The end will come with a **flood**, and war and its miseries are decreed from that time to the very end." (Daniel 9:26)(emphasis added)* Some try to spiritualise the flood but it seems clear that it's a literal description. However, not even this will harm the faithful evacuees. A crack of some description in the earth's surface will drain the water away and this will help God's people complete their escape.

Frustrated, Satan will instead turn his attention to the *"rest of her children - all who keep God's commandments and maintain their testimony for Jesus."* Who are the rest of Israel's children? Well, it seems as though the 144,000 would have been witnessing and making converts during the trumpets. The two witnesses, who will stay in Jerusalem during this time, are also probably making converts. So the believers will continue to grow on earth through their efforts. It's these that Satan goes after. It's these who Jesus was talking about when he said, *"In fact, unless that time of calamity is shortened, not a single person will survive. But it will be shortened for the sake of God's chosen ones."* (Matt 24:22)

What about the Antichrist himself though? What kind of man will he be? Where will he come from? The answers are right ahead.

## THE ANTICHRIST

*"Then I saw a beast rising up out of the sea. It had seven heads and ten horns, with ten crowns on its horns. And written on each head were names that blasphemed God. This beast looked like a leopard, but it had the feet of a bear and the mouth of a lion! And the dragon gave the beast his own power and throne and great authority."* (Rev 13:1-3)

The sea prophetically represents the mass of godless people of the world. God told Isaiah, *"But those who still reject me are like the restless sea, which is never still but continually churns up* mud and dirt." (Isaiah 57:20) So the Antichrist will be a Gentile who will come out of the 'sea' of the world's godless people.

Isaiah may narrow his nationality down still further. In his writings we see a description of an Assyrian whose characteristics very closely match those of the Antichrist: *"What sorrow awaits Assyria, the rod of my anger. I use it as a club to express my anger. I am sending Assyria against a godless nation, against a people with whom I am angry. Assyria will plunder them, trampling them like dirt beneath its feet. But the king of Assyria will not understand that he is my tool; his mind does not work that way. His plan is simply to destroy, to cut down nation after nation." (Isaiah 10:5-7)*

This passage tells us that the Assyrian will cut down "nation after nation" i.e. the world at first (via the 200 million?), but then more specifically, he will be used by God to conquer Israel (Israel is the godless nation that God is angry with here). He is allowing the Assyrian to trample on Israel to fulfil his wrath against them. However, the Assyrian doesn't realise that God is ultimately still in control. The Assyrian believes he is doing it all in his own strength. As such, he is described as being proud, arrogant and boastful. In fact, he believes himself to be invincible. Isaiah writes, *"he is proud and arrogant. He boasts, "By my own powerful arm I have done this. With my own shrewd wisdom I planned it. I have broken down the defences of nations and carried off their treasures. I have knocked down their kings like a bull. I have robbed their nests of riches and gathered up kingdoms as a farmer gathers eggs. No one can even flap a wing against me or utter a peep of protest." (Isaiah 10:12-14)*

Assyria doesn't exist today but around the time that Isaiah was written, they had an empire that primarily covered the areas of modern Turkey, Syria, Iraq and Western Iran - the four nations around the Euphrates that were brought to our attention during the fifth trumpet. We must also note that the Assyrian empire spread to places like Jordan, Lebanon, Kuwait and even touched Northern parts of Egypt and Saudi Arabia. If I had to be specific though, I would suggest that he will come from Syria. And I'll explain the reasons later.

What about this odd description of the beast? *"It had seven heads and ten horns, with ten crowns on its horns. And written on each head were names that blasphemed God. This beast looked like a leopard, but it had the feet of a bear and the mouth of a lion! And the dragon gave the beast his own power and throne and great authority."* What kind of bizarre creature will the Antichrist be?

Well again, this is just prophetic imagery. Don't expect him to literally look like a leopard/lion/bear hybrid. In order to translate this image, we must first notice the similarities with the earlier description of the dragon, which was also said to have *"seven heads and ten horns."(Rev 12:3)* This tells us that the Antichrist will be the very image of Satan on earth. In the same way that Jesus Christ was the very image of God.

As for insight into the meaning of the animals, we can find some if we turn to Daniel. We're going on a bit of a detour here but I'll try to keep it as simple as possible:

*"Earlier, during the first year of King Belshazzar's reign in Babylon, Daniel had a dream and saw visions as he lay in his bed. He wrote down the dream, and this is what he saw.*

*In my vision that night, I, Daniel, saw a great storm churning the surface of a great sea, with strong winds blowing from every direction. Then four huge beasts came up out of the water, each different from the others.*

*The first beast was like a lion with eagles' wings. As I watched, its wings were pulled off, and it was left standing with its two hind feet on the ground, like a human being. And it was given a human mind.*

*Then I saw a second beast, and it looked like a bear. It was rearing up on one side, and it had three ribs in its mouth between its teeth. And I heard a voice saying to it, "Get up! Devour the flesh of many people!"*

*Then the third of these strange beasts appeared, and it looked like a leopard. It had four bird's wings on its back, and it had four heads. Great authority was given to this beast.*

*Then in my vision that night, I saw a fourth beast—terrifying, dreadful, and very strong. It devoured and crushed its victims with huge iron teeth and trampled their remains beneath its feet. It was different from any of the other beasts, and it had ten horns."*

*As I was looking at the horns, suddenly another small horn appeared among them. Three of the first horns were torn out by the roots to make room for it. This little horn had eyes like human eyes and a mouth that was boasting arrogantly.*

*I watched as thrones were put in place*
*   and the Ancient One sat down to judge.*
*His clothing was as white as snow,*

*his hair like purest wool.*
*He sat on a fiery throne*
*    with wheels of blazing fire,*
*and a river of fire was pouring out,*
*    flowing from his presence.*
*Millions of angels ministered to him;*
*    many millions stood to attend him.*
*Then the court began its session,*
*    and the books were opened.*

(NB: this intermission describing God holding court tells us that this event is taking place during the Day of God's Judgement or Wrath.)

*I continued to watch because I could hear the little horn's boastful speech. I kept watching until the fourth beast was killed and its body was destroyed by fire. The other three beasts had their authority taken from them, but they were allowed to live a while longer.*

*As my vision continued that night, I saw someone like a son of man coming with the clouds of heaven. He approached the Ancient One and was led into his presence. He was given authority, honour, and sovereignty over all the nations of the world, so that people of every race and nation and language would obey him. His rule is eternal—it will never end. His kingdom will never be destroyed." (Daniel 7:1-14)*

The details of this vision could still be quite puzzling but thankfully Daniel asked for clarification on what he had just seen:

*"I, Daniel, was troubled by all I had seen, and my visions terrified me. So I approached one of those standing beside the throne and asked him what it all meant. He explained it to me like this "These four huge beasts represent four kingdoms that will arise from the earth. But in the end, the holy people of the Most High will be given the kingdom, and they will rule forever and ever."*

*Then I wanted to know the true meaning of the fourth beast, the one so different from the others and so terrifying. It had devoured and crushed its victims with iron teeth and bronze claws, trampling their remains beneath its feet. I also asked about the ten horns on the fourth beast's head and the little horn that came up afterward and destroyed three of the other horns. This horn had seemed greater than the others, and it had human eyes and a mouth that was boasting arrogantly. As I watched, this horn was waging war against God's holy people and was defeating them, until the Ancient One—the Most High—came and judged in favour of his holy people. Then the time arrived for the holy people to take over the kingdom.*

*Then he said to me, "This fourth beast is the fourth world power that will rule the earth. It will be different from all the others. It will devour the whole world, trampling and crushing everything in its path. Its ten horns are ten kings who will rule that empire. Then another king will arise, different from the other ten, who will subdue three of them. He will defy the Most High and oppress the holy people of the Most High. He will try to change their sacred festivals and laws, and they will be placed under his control for a time, times, and half a time." (Daniel 7:15-25)*

So to simplify, Daniel is told that four empires would arise from the earth. The first three would have a period of dominance but none would compare to the fourth, which is an end-time kingdom that would somehow encapsulate or incorporate the previous three, either literally or in essence, and in doing so, would devour the whole world. In other words, the fourth kingdom would be the world's first truly global empire. It would be a one world government.

Under this system, the world will be divided into ten regions and each region will be led by its own ruler. This is represented in the image by the ten horns with ten crowns. However, one man (a little horn) will rise up from within this system of governance and he will come to overrule them all. He will particularly subdue three rulers (horns), who would appear to be resistant to his authority and ultimately he will become the most powerful man in the world. A kind of global dictator. This is the Antichrist. So you'll notice that when the Bible is talking about this fourth beast, it's talking about an empire on the one hand, but it's also talking about the "little horn" who dominates this empire. Therefore, it gives him human characteristics. It says he has human eyes and a human mouth and can make boastful speeches. It also tells us that he is the one causing Jacob's Trouble by *"waging war against God's holy people and...defeating them, until the Ancient One—the Most High— came and judged in favour of his holy people."* The Antichrist will rule this final global empire right up until the return of the Most High - Jesus Christ.

This description of four consecutive empires that culminates in an end-time global empire ruled by the Antichrist was revealed to Daniel in another way - through a dream that King Nebuchadnezzar of Babylon had. Daniel tells the king what he saw and then interprets:

*"In your vision, Your Majesty, you saw standing before you a huge, shining statue of a man. It was a frightening sight. The head of the statue was made of fine gold. Its chest and arms were silver, its belly and thighs were bronze, its legs were iron, and its feet were a combination of iron and baked clay. As you watched, a rock was cut from a mountain, but not by human hands. It struck the feet of iron and clay, smashing them to bits. The whole statue was crushed into small pieces of iron, clay, bronze, silver, and gold. Then the wind blew them away without a trace, like chaff on a threshing floor. But the rock that knocked the statue down became a great mountain that covered the whole earth.*

*"That was the dream. Now we will tell the king what it means. Your Majesty, you are the greatest of kings. The God of heaven has given you sovereignty, power, strength, and honour. He has made you the ruler over all the inhabited world and has put even the wild animals and birds under your control. You are the head of gold.*

*"But after your kingdom comes to an end, another kingdom, inferior to yours, will rise to take your place. After that kingdom has fallen, yet a third kingdom, represented by bronze, will rise to rule the world. Following that kingdom, there will be a fourth one, as strong as iron. That kingdom will smash and crush all previous empires, just as iron smashes and crushes everything it strikes. The feet and toes you saw were a combination of iron and baked clay, showing that this kingdom will be divided. Like iron mixed with clay, it will have some of the strength of iron. But while some parts of it will be as strong as iron, other parts will be as weak as clay. This mixture of iron and clay also shows that these kingdoms will try to strengthen themselves by*

*forming alliances with each other through intermarriage. But they will not hold together, just as iron and clay do not mix.*

*"During the reigns of those kings, the God of heaven will set up a kingdom that will never be destroyed or conquered. It will crush all these kingdoms into nothingness, and it will stand forever. That is the meaning of the rock cut from the mountain, though not by human hands, that crushed to pieces the statue of iron, bronze, clay, silver, and gold. The great God was showing the king what will happen in the future. The dream is true, and its meaning is certain." (Daniel 2:31-45)*

Again we see a succession of four kingdoms - this time represented by a statue - with the fourth and final one being a global empire with ten rulers...represented by ten toes at the feet of the statue. The nations of the world will try to form alliances at this time for unity and even though that endeavour won't be an unqualified success, the empire will surpass all the previous great empires. It will remain on earth until Jesus Christ himself - the rock not cut from human hands - smashes it to pieces and then sets up his own kingdom on earth.

Its important to note that the Antichrist's global empire can be destroyed no other way. You see, historically, when *national* dictators have come to the fore, there have always been other national leaders to fight back and defeat them. For every Hitler there has been a Churchill. However, if a *global* political structure with a *global* constitution is put in place, and if a global dictator rises to the top of *that* system, and if that dictator therefore has control of the entire planet's assets, intelligence databases and military machinery, there will be no human entity left to stand against the tyranny. We'd be looking for someone from outside this world to rescue us. That's why the Bible says the end-time empire will not be smashed by any human army, but by Jesus Christ himself upon his second coming. When he does so, all traces of the four kingdoms will disappear and he will then establish his own rule throughout the earth.

Can we be specific about what these four kingdoms represent?

## THE FOUR KINGDOMS

Many people argue about what the four kingdoms represent in the belief that identifying the first three historical kingdoms will help us identify the prophetic fourth kingdom from afar. I don't necessarily buy into that theory. I think that when the leaders of the world decide we need a one world government that divides the world into ten regions with ten rulers, it's going to be blatantly obvious to any believers on earth at that time that the prophetic structure is being put in place for the Antichrist's appearance. In other words, regardless of what we believe the previous three kingdoms to be, the fourth is going to be such an unmissable fulfilment of prophecy that our interpretations of the previous three won't actually matter too much.

And indeed, you'll notice that Daniel doesn't seem to be much interested in the first three kingdoms either. He just wants to know why this fourth beast looks so much different from the rest. That's his focus.

Having said that, it's worth looking at the various theories that have been put forward regarding the four kingdoms:

The classic view of the four kingdoms is that the first gold head or lion kingdom is Babylon, the second bear kingdom is Medo-Persia, the third leopard kingdom is Greece and the fourth kingdom of iron is Rome. Babylon is specifically identified as the head of gold by Daniel so there's not much to debate there. The Medes and Persians then invaded Babylon and that's represented by the chest with two arms. Next the Greek Empire started off unified but was divided into two after the death of Alexander the Great. That's signified by the belly of the statue dividing into two thighs. The fourth kingdom of Rome then had two centres: Rome in the West and Constantinople in the East. Hence, the two iron legs on the statue. Since the feet of the statue also contains iron mixed with clay, it is therefore believed that the Roman empire will be resurrected in the end-times. This theory obviously places a great deal of suspicion on the European Union (which was initiated with the Treaty of Rome) and perhaps the Catholic church.

A second school of thought, which could be termed the Western perspective, says that Great Britain has always been represented by a lion and the United States has always been represented by an eagle. So when the Bible talks about the first empire as *"a lion with eagles' wings"* and then says, *"its wings were pulled off"*, we can't help but notice that the United States was once a British colony - the two countries were once connected - and that after the American Declaration of Independence in 1776, when the lion had its wings pulled off, so to speak, Britain went on to establish the largest empire in world history. This view hits a snag however, when we consider that Daniel already specifically identifies the first kingdom as Babylon - not Britain.

That should kill this theory stone dead but for the sake of the argument, let's go on to consider that this perspective then says that the second bear kingdom is Russia. And indeed, since at least the 19th century, the bear has tended to symbolise Russia. After the Second World War, Communist Russia took control of what became known as the Eastern Block - countries including Poland, Hungary, Czechoslovakia, Romania, Albania and East Germany. These all became Soviet Socialist Republics. The Communism of Russia also found allies further abroad in places like China, Cuba and North Korea. Theirs was an empire of ideology. Perhaps most significantly, in the aftermath of World War II, Alger Hiss, an assistant to American President Franklin D Roosevelt, was chosen to draft the charter for the United Nations. Alger Hiss was later accused and convicted of being a Communist spy. In other words, the charter for the United Nations was written by a cohort of Joseph Stalin. The United Nations was initiated with the idea of forming a global socialist government.

What about the third kingdom that *"looked like a leopard"* and which *"had four bird's wings on its back, and it had four heads"*? The leopard is most closely associated with Germany while the national symbol of France is a rooster. This places us in Europe. The four heads could be explained by the fact that there have been four successive "reichs" in Europe. Firstly, there was the Holy Roman Empire, then the Germanic Empire which began under Otto Von Bismarck, then the third Reich of Adolf Hitler, and then finally, once it became clear that Germany was going to be defeated in World War II, the European Union was initiated and effectively accomplished by diplomacy what Hitler had failed to achieve through war - a united Europe dominated by Germany with no borders and a single currency. The

European Union is indeed now completely dominated by a Franco-German alliance with all those advantages in place.

This Western perspective therefore, is that the final global empire will somehow incorporate the ideas, essence and character of these previous empires involving Rome, Britain, America, Germany, France, Russia, the European Union and United Nations. World leaders will decide that by dividing the whole earth into ten regions and establishing a supreme council of ten rulers over those regions, as part of a one world government, this will represent the best opportunity for bringing lasting peace and stability to the earth. However, with that geopolitical structure in place - no doubt ratified by a new global constitution - it will only take one man, empowered by Satan himself, to dominate and subdue the other leaders and to effectively become a global dictator.

Finally, there's the Eastern view.

Eastern scholars say that God never concerns himself prophetically with Europe or the West and that end-time prophecy focuses entirely on the Middle East (see Appendix 3). Therefore, they would say that the lion represents Babylon (Iraq), the bear represents Persia (Iran)...up until this point they agree with the classic view....but then they deviate and say that the third leopard kingdom represents the Ottoman Empire of the Turks. They believe that the fourth world empire will therefore be an Islamic one that comes out of those fifth trumpet nations by the Euphrates. And since Iraq, Iran and Turkey have already had their day as empire capitals, they believe the fourth empire will be based in Syria. Most likely Damascus. That's where the Assyrian Antichrist is likely to come from in their view.

Is there any evidence that the Muslims are working towards building a new empire? Quite a lot actually. In fact, it's no secret that Muslims are trying to establish a kind of United States of Islam under one spiritual leader.

The Islamic word for "empire" is "caliphate" and although they haven't had a caliphate recently, they have had several in the past. During Muhammad's life they were united under his rule (570-632AD). Immediately after him came the Rashidun caliphate (632-661AD). That was succeeded by the Umayyad caliphate (662-750AD). Following that came the Abbasid caliphate (750-1258AD). Finally, the most recent, the largest, and perhaps the most well-known Islamic caliphate was the Ottoman Empire based in Turkey. It ended on March 3rd, 1924.[1]

Ever since the ending of the Ottoman Empire, Muslims have fundamentally been in disarray, divided by factions and in-fighting. All the while, as they see it, "the dark shadow of the West has engulfed the world." They believe that the 20th Century saw Western capitalism and liberalism bringing "chaos, inequality, despotism and international disorder". They believe the only solution for the whole planet is a new Islamic caliphate. According to Islamic prophecy, they believe the next caliphate will indeed be a global one, and that it will be ushered in by the "12th Imam" or Al Mahdi (Muslim Messiah). They believe this man will be a direct descendant of Muhammad and thus, will be able to unify the Islamic world. In their prophetic writings, they see all the Islamic nations deferring ultimate authority to him as he wages war on the West, defeating it, imposing Shariah law, and reigning unchallenged for seven years over a global empire.[2]

You can read about the Muslim plan for an end-time caliphate by going to http://www.khilafah.com - the site from which the quotes in the previous paragraph were taken. When we consider how the Muslim Brotherhood are currently trying to consolidate authority throughout the Islamic world by agitating uprisings and revolutions in the Middle East, we can see that their long-term intention is to create the necessary conditions for the Mahdi and his Islamic empire. The Arab Spring won't lead to freedom and democracy; it well lead to the political domination of Islam in the Middle East.

When we compare all the views of the end-time kingdom - classic, Western and Eastern - they all have merits. There may even be some truth in all of them. I would suggest that it will go something like this:

All world leaders will willingly work to create a global political structure which joins nations together and centralises authority. We've already seen projects like this embodied in the European Union and the United Nations. We've also seen organisations like the G8 and G20 rise to prominence and this is underpinned by a desire for greater cohesion in solving global issues...global warming, global security, the global economy etc. Indeed, politicians, the super-rich elite, spiritual gurus and members of secret societies have been talking about creating a One World Order for many years. This will all lead to a time when a global constitution will come into play that all nation states will sign up to believing it to be the path to world peace and prosperity. The earth will then be divided into ten regions and a council of ten leaders will be appointed to rule each of those regions. This global empire will obviously require Middle Eastern representation. And since Muslims will have been busy wiping out Christians and consolidating their power in that region, the world council representative for the Middle East will probably be Muslim. Because of political correctness and spiritual blindness, we would expect the leaders in Europe and the West to support that - especially if the man in question initially presents himself as a peaceful 'moderate' or even hides his spiritual allegiance altogether. All it would then take is for that man to unveil his true identity once in power, (or for a successor to come along after him) unite the Islamic world as their Messianic Mahdi, send out the call for the army of 200 million to gather so that Islamic prophecy might be fulfilled, and from that region wipe out a third of the world's population. Having conquered many nations and having taken advantage of the new global political structure, he will finally turn on Israel - the nation that causes the greatest affront to the Muslim mind. Jacob's Trouble will begin and the true nature of this man as the Antichrist will be revealed. This is indeed how Islamic prophecy itself predicts the 'last hour':

*"The Last Hour would not come unless the Muslims will fight against the Jews. The Jews would hide themselves behind a stone or a tree and a stone or a tree would say: 'Muslim, or the servant of Allah, there is a Jew behind me; come and kill him;' but the tree Gharqad would not say, for it is the tree of the Jews." (Sahih Muslim, Kitab al-Fitan wa Ashrat as-Sa'ah, Book 41, 6985)*

In other words, I believe the framework of the One World Order will be established by all the world leaders, but it will be hi-jacked from within by the Antichrist.

Whatever our thoughts about the first three kingdoms, I will repeat that Daniel actually pays very little attention to them -

it's the fourth that really intrigues him. And whatever identity we attach to the previous three, it doesn't really affect the obvious nature of the fourth. An empire. Global. Ten rulers. Dominated by one. Comes in peace. Turns violent. Earth subdued first. Israel attacked second. We'll know it when we see it.

## THE ANTICHRIST'S RULE

With that detour over, we now have a picture of the kind of circumstances into which the Antichrist will come to power. Let's turn back to Revelation now where John gives us some more details:

*"I saw that one of the heads of the beast seemed wounded beyond recovery—but the fatal wound was healed! The whole world marvelled at this miracle and gave allegiance to the beast. They worshiped the dragon for giving the beast such power, and they also worshiped the beast. "Who is as great as the beast?" they exclaimed. "Who is able to fight against him?" (Rev 13:1-4)*

The Antichrist will mimic Jesus by appearing to suffer a fatal wound and then being healed. This trick resurrection is going to cause the world to marvel at his apparent supernatural powers of recovery. They will pledge allegiance to him and by proxy, pledge allegiance to Satan - the one empowering him. This event will add to the Antichrist's air of invincibility and the whole world will exclaim, *"Who is able to fight against him?"* Remember the Assyrian held a similarly high view of himself boasting, *"No one can even flap a wing against me or utter a peep of protest"*. So when the whole world unites under him, even the nations who don't particularly like him will have no strength to fight against him. His position will be unassailable.

*"Then the beast was allowed to speak great blasphemies against God. And he was given authority to do whatever he wanted for forty-two months. And he spoke terrible words of blasphemy against God, slandering his name and his dwelling—that is, those who dwell in heaven. And the beast was allowed to wage war against God's holy people and to conquer them. And he was given authority to rule over every tribe and people and language and nation. And all the people who belong to this world worshiped the beast. They are the ones whose names were not written in the Book of Life before the world was made—the Book that belongs to the Lamb who was slaughtered.*

*Anyone with ears to hear*
*should listen and understand.*
*Anyone who is destined for prison*
*will be taken to prison.*
*Anyone destined to die by the sword*
*will die by the sword.*

*This means that God's holy people must endure persecution patiently and remain faithful." (Rev 13:5-10)*

Here we are told again that the Antichrist will be *"given authority to do whatever he wanted for forty-two months."* Unfortunately, "whatever he wants" will be to crush Jerusalem and anyone who turns to God. It's Jacob's Trouble again. This passage also confirms that his dominion will be worldwide. He will *"rule over every tribe and people and language and nation."* It will truly be a global empire.

Remember what happened when Jesus was being tempted in the wilderness? *"Next the devil took [Jesus] to the peak of a very high mountain and showed him all the kingdoms of the world and their glory. "I will give it all to you," he said, "if you will kneel down and worship me." (Matt 4:8-9)* Jesus, the Christ, turned Satan down. This man will not. He will accept Satan's offer and become ruler of *all* the kingdoms of the world. He's basically driven by selfish ambition - a trait that can be seen in many of our political leaders today. And he has a special hatred for God's most precious possession - Jerusalem.

During this time the Antichrist will blaspheme God and even set himself up as God. I find it interesting that he will also speak against all *"those who dwell in heaven"* too. Clearly Satan is sore about his recent defeat at their hands and with his pride bruised, is slandering his conquerors at every opportunity.

## WHO IS THE ANTICHRIST?

You'll often hear people speculating about the exact identity of the Antichrist today. Indeed, throughout history, it's almost been a past-time for Christians to speculate on the identity of the Antichrist. And again, because people tend to view prophecy through the lens of current events, almost every unpopular political or religious leader for centuries has been touted as a potential candidate. As I write in late 2013, Barak Obama is doing incredibly unpopular things in the United States and so the latest fad is to pin the tag on him. But before him, Bill Clinton was tagged as the Antichrist. (In fact, most Democrat Presidents are given the title at some point.) Henry Kissinger had it for a while. Mikhail Gorbachev did too. Hitler and Stalin were obvious candidates. Napoleon. Bill Gates. Prince Charles.

Prince William. Jacques Chirac. The list is almost endless. We have to lift ourselves above the clamour and sensationalistic noise of current events and become a little more far-sighted than that. Barak Obama is a bad president to be sure - there may even be good cause to call him an antichrist by the Biblical definition as one who denies the Son - but he is not *the* Antichrist. Just as Clinton and Kissinger and the rest weren't. We can't keep crying wolf every time an unpopular leader comes along like this because it discredits the truth that the Antichrist *is* coming.[3]

God has clearly set out the circumstances under which the Antichrist will rise and we know that those circumstances haven't arrived. We don't have a truly global system of governance yet. We're getting there slowly...but not yet. The third temple hasn't been built yet either. Or even commissioned. Indeed, a lot of prophecy needs to find fulfilment before we'll know who he is. Yes, *many* little antichrists will come before that point and already, many of them have come and gone. Hitler was probably the closest to the end-time Antichrist that we've seen so far. We'll see many more in the future too. But, quite scarily, none of them compare to the one to come. That one who is the embodiment of Satan himself.

During the Antichrist's 42 month reign when his power and authority will be absolute, God will expect his followers to persevere once again saying, *"Anyone who is destined for prison will be taken to prison. Anyone destined to die by the sword will die by the sword. This means that God's holy people must endure persecution patiently and remain faithful." (Rev 13:10)*

So again we see that God won't necessarily spare all his followers this persecution. Some people are destined to suffer and die for him. The 144,000 are safe in the wilderness but those who are left behind will have to count the cost. Dietrich Bonhoeffer once said that *"When Christ calls a man, he bids him come and die."* This is clearly a message that we get from Revelation. God is looking for men and women who, *"...did not love their lives so much that they were afraid to die." (Rev 12:11)* When Jesus told us that godless people would do to us what they had done to him, we must take that promise seriously. Many will be forced to walk that road behind the Saviour and die, just as he died, at the hands of enemies. However, the Bible reminds us that to retain faith even in the face of that prospect is to be considered victorious in God's eyes. And there will be great rewards for such bravery.

*"If you cling to your life, you will lose it, and if you let your life go, you will save it." (Luke 17:33)*

## THE FALSE PROPHET

The Antichrist has another beside him who helps to consolidate his authority - a false prophet. He is described as coming out of the earth:

*"Then I saw another beast come up out of the earth. He had two horns like those of a lamb, but he spoke with the voice of a dragon. He exercised all the authority of the first beast. And he required all the earth and its people to worship the first beast, whose fatal wound had been healed. He did astounding miracles, even making fire flash down to earth from the sky*

*while everyone was watching. And with all the miracles he was allowed to perform on behalf of the first beast, he deceived all the people who belong to this world. He ordered the people to make a great statue of the first beast, who was fatally wounded and then came back to life. He was then permitted to give life to this statue so that it could speak. Then the statue of the beast commanded that anyone refusing to worship it must die." (Rev 13:11-15)*

If the Antichrist is controlled directly by Satan, I believe this false prophet will be controlled directly by Abaddon, The Destroyer. Here, the False Prophet is described as the beast that comes out of the earth and we know that Abaddon was the evil spirit who came out of the earth - the bottomless pit. Furthermore, you'll remember that the two witnesses are going to be killed by the beast from the bottomless pit, so we know that Abaddon will be prominent and full of authority during this time of Jacob's Trouble. That's why I believe the two witnesses will actually be killed by the False Prophet, under Abaddon's control, or even possession.

The False Prophet appears to generally act as a right-hand man to the Antichrist. He consolidates the Antichrist's authority, directs people to worship the Antichrist and operates with all the authority of the Antichrist. The Bible tells us that he will have the outward appearance of a lamb - in other words, the appearance of Christ - but he will speak with the mouth of the dragon - Satan. Appearances will definitely be deceiving.

One of his most significant acts will be to *"make a great statue of the first beast"*. This idol of the Antichrist is the 'Abomination of Desolation' or the 'sacrilegious object that causes desecration' that will be set up in the rebuilt Temple. He will command everyone to worship it or die. And remember, the establishing of this idol will mark the beginning of the final 42 months of his reign.

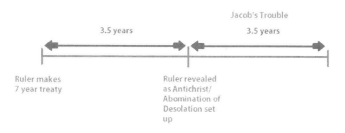

Jesus said, "*"The day is coming when you will see what Daniel the prophet spoke about—the sacrilegious object that causes desecration standing in the Holy Place." (Reader, pay attention!) "Then those in Judea must flee to the hills. A person out on the deck of a roof must not go down into the house to pack. A person out in the field must not return even to get a coat. How terrible it will be for pregnant women and for nursing mothers in those days. And pray that your flight will not be in winter or on the Sabbath. For there will be greater anguish than at any time since the world began. And it will never be so great again. In fact, unless that time of calamity is shortened, not a single person will survive. But it will be shortened for the sake of God's chosen ones."*

*"Then if anyone tells you, 'Look, here is the Messiah,' or 'There he is,' don't believe it. For false messiahs and false prophets will rise up and perform great signs and wonders so as to deceive, if*

*possible, even God's chosen ones. See, I have warned you about this ahead of time." (Matt 24:15-25)*

Notice how Jesus says that if anyone comes along during this time claiming to be a Messiah or a prophet, not to believe them. This is because it's exactly during this time that the Antichrist *will* come along claiming to be a Messiah and it *will* be during this time that the False Prophet establishes the Abomination of Desolation on Temple Mount. Jesus is telling us not to get involved with these two.

The False Prophet will be able to back up his claims with miracles and this will be a strong delusion for many. He'll even be able to make *"fire flash down to earth from the sky while everyone was watching."(Rev 13:13)* In this way, he will mimic Jesus who was able to command the natural elements when the storm came upon the Sea of Galilee (Mark 4:35-41). Remember, Satan is able to perform miracles too. Supernatural signs and wonders are not automatic proof of godliness. And indeed, lying signs and wonders will be on the increase in the years to come.

A final interesting point to make about the False Prophet from this passage is that he will have the power to *"give life to this statue so that it could speak."* How will he be able to animate the idolatrous Abomination of Desolation in such a way that it can talk? Again, I believe this will become increasingly clear as we move closer to the time.

Imagine if I had told my great-grandmother, living in the 19th Century, that the whole world would be able to simultaneously watch live sporting events happening on another continent through an electronic screen in the living room, or that scientists would be able to clone animals, or that we would be able to send electronic mail from one part of the globe to another in the blink of an eye using a device that could fit in our pocket, or that we could genetically modify plants...her mind would be blown at the thought. In a world of horse-drawn carriages, such things would have been inconceivable - beyond her wildest imagination. In a similar way, although technological advances are starting to give us an idea of how an inanimate object can be given life (just recently I read about scientists growing creatures from cells in an artificial womb),  I believe there will be still further quantum leaps forward in the fields of biotechnology and cybernetics. Indeed, the rate at which scientific knowledge is increasing is one of the most striking hallmarks of our era. And this fits with what Daniel was told about the end-times:

*"But you, Daniel, keep this prophecy a secret; seal up the book until the time of the end, when many will rush here and there, and knowledge will increase." (Daniel 12:4)*

The Greek word for "knowledge" is "science." He is being told that life would become increasingly fast-paced and full of scientific breakthroughs. Certainly this prophecy is coming true in the world today.

The False Prophet's ability to animate an idol will mimic God as the Creator of life. And although we can't say for certain right now how he will do that, it will be simply unmistakeable when it happens. A giant idol of a global leader in a rebuilt third temple which is capable of speech amidst a ruined Israel under a one world government is going to be front page news. Again, God hasn't left us without blatantly obvious signs.

What's interesting about Daniel's prophecy of Jacob's Trouble, is that he is the only one to point to a period *after* the 1,260 days. And it's measured from the moment the Abomination of Desolation is set up. Daniel is told, *"From the time the daily sacrifice is stopped and the sacrilegious object that causes desecration is set up to be worshiped, there will be 1,290 days. And blessed are those who wait and remain until the end of the 1,335 days!" (Daniel 12:11-12)*

So the establishing of this idol is an important time-marker. We already know that from the moment it is set up, the Antichrist will reign unchallenged for 1,260 days, but here Daniel is told there will another 30 days (1 month) of life on earth beyond that reign. And then another month and a half (45 days) beyond that...making 1,335 days in total.

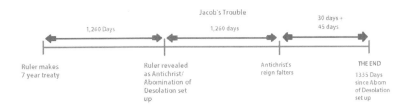

We'll get to the significance of the last 45 days later but for now, the Bible isn't quite finished telling us about the Antichrist, the False Prophet and Jacob's Trouble.

Next it tells us about the economic system that will be in place during this time.

## THE ECONOMIC SYSTEM

*"He required everyone—small and great, rich and poor, free and slave—to be given a mark on the right hand or on the forehead. And no one could buy or sell anything without that mark, which was either the name of the beast or the number representing his name. Wisdom is needed here. Let the one with understanding solve the meaning of the number of the beast, for it is the number of a man. His number is 666." (Rev 13:16-18)*

In many countries the right-hand man to the President or Prime Minister is the man who runs the economy - the Chancellor. So it's not surprising that, in what is perhaps the best known passage of Revelation, we are told that the False Prophet, on behalf of the Antichrist's one world government, will initiate an economy controlled by a mark that is placed on the right hand or on the forehead.

Nobody will be able to buy or sell without this mark. Which means nobody will be able to participate in society without the mark. If you can't buy or sell then you can't own a business, sell products or services, buy food, buy clothes, pay a mortgage or rent a property, drive a car, get on the bus, gain employment, buy insurance, own a passport, pay taxes or really do anything at all. If you don't join this system then your destiny is living in caves, hunting and foraging for nuts and berries and trying to avoid detection from the authorities who will put you in prison or kill you if they find you. We know that the 144,000 will be surviving in the wilderness during this time but only because they have the special favour of God. It won't be so easy for the rest.

We don't really need to speculate as to how the mark of the beast could be implemented because the technology already exists. In fact, it has already been trialled. For some time now, we have been moving towards a cashless society. Globally, cash transactions are still the most popular method of payment but the rise of electronic payments seems to be unstoppable. In the *World Payments Report 2013*, it was revealed that global debit card usage is going up by about 15.8% per year, credit card usage is going up by about 12.3% per year, online payments are expected to rise by 18.1% next year (2014) and mobile phone payments are expected to rise by a massive 58.5%. Total non-cash payments are expected to top 333 billion per year in 2013. Kevin Brown, global head of transaction services at RBS International Banking sums it up when he says, *"The unabated rise of non-cash payments is a sign of the interconnected lives we live today...nearly 47 transactions per year are carried out for every man, woman and child on the planet."[4]*

Significantly, we're also seeing a trend towards contactless payments. Debit and credit cards have long been fitted with "Chip and PIN" capabilities but now they're also being installed with integrated RFID chips. These new chips emit a radio frequency capable of communicating with payment processing devices up to a range 5 metres away.

All new smartphones are able to send and receive money through contactless NFC (Near Field Communication) technology too. Banks are increasingly aware of their customer's desire to pay for goods and services though their mobile phones and are producing banking and "wallet" apps that contain those capabilities. As these forms of payment become increasingly ubiquitous, the drawbacks of cash are becoming obvious. Cash is less secure, it's dirty, it's not traceable, it's risky and costly to transport, it takes more time to count and process...and let's not even consider cheques. It has already been announced by UK banks that cheques are being phased out and will become completely obsolete within a couple of years. On the other hand, what could be simpler than secure, wireless, electronic transfers that take 0.001 seconds for a computer to process?

From contactless payment technology incorporated into debit cards and mobile phones, it's a very small leap to transfer that pre-existing, ubiquitous, easy, quick, efficient system into an even more secure environment - the human body itself. For many years, the existence of the Verichip has been well known. This is a chip about the size of a grain of rice that can be implanted under the skin and which is capable of storing all the necessary details required for payment transactions, along with other identifiers such Social Security or National Insurance numbers, medical records and such like. In trials they even discovered that the most efficient place to implant this chip was in the wrist or forehead. Upon the invention of this chip, a future was painted whereby we could live entirely without wallets, credit cards, ID cards, passports, loose change or any kind of money whatsoever.

When you go to the supermarket, imagine if the chip in your wrist could automatically communicate with the store's checkout computer and the money could be debited from your account without having to rummage around for cards or money? Quick, hassle free shopping. No need for PIN codes or passwords and it's more secure too. After all, people may lose their cards and phones all the time but it takes a special set of circumstances to lose a wrist or a head!

We already know about some of the other benefits of this system because we're already utilising them. For example, in many countries it's now illegal to own a pet that hasn't been microchipped. The benefits of chipping animals are clear. When they get lost, they can be scanned and instantly the animal's name, address and vaccination records are available to the vet or the finder who can then return the pet safely. Some pets now even have chips which communicate with doors so that they will automatically open when the animal approaches. Others are now being implanted with GPS chips that relay their location to an owner who is able to pick it up on their mobile device. No more getting lost! There's no reason why similar benefits wouldn't apply to children, or to people in general.

Indeed, many in the medical profession are already pushing for people to be chipped. They complain that when they arrive on the scene of an accident and can't communicate with the injured party, they are forced to operate 'blind'. In other words, first responders and surgeons don't know about allergies, medical histories, blood types etc. and this puts them at a disadvantage in knowing how to treat the injuries effectively and safely. However, imagine if all that data was stored in a chip that could be scanned by the first responder team or by the nurses at the hospital. Right away this gives them a jump start on how to proceed. It could even tell them if the patient has a history of alcoholism or any drug convictions.

And then there are the security benefits. We've already had politicians trying to foist ID cards on the general population in a bid to foil terrorism. The same arguments could be used to foist biometric technology on us. Indeed, we're already seeing tech companies introducing biometrics into their products. Apple led the way with fingerprint scanning on the iPhone 5s and other smartphone manufacturers have followed suit. Supermarket giants, Tesco, have recently announced that they will be trialling OptimEyes eyeball and face recognition scanners so that they can tailor advertising to shoppers at the checkouts while they wait - technology similar to that seen in the movie, Minority Report.[5] Imagine if they could tailor the adverts based on the information contained within your personal biochip? That's something they would be very interested in.

So as the whole world amalgamates and fears about terrorism and identity theft rise, and as the arguments from scientists, politicians, doctors and bankers are put forward, and as corporations learn that this technology could serve their commercial interests, and as the technology itself increasingly makes this all possible, we can clearly see a route through which the various interests will converge to make this happen in the end-time kingdom. Especially when despotic authorities realise it will give them an easy way to track our movements and activities.

"But an implantable microchip can't be the mark of the beast. The mark of the beast must be a visible mark!" This is a common argument.  So it's interesting that scientists are currently developing "epidermal electronics" or "data tattoos". These are basically microchips that are tattooed onto the skin. Ironically enough, the developers of this technology at Coleman Labs decided to demonstrate their capabilities by specifically illustrating how they can be utilised on the forehead or the wrist.

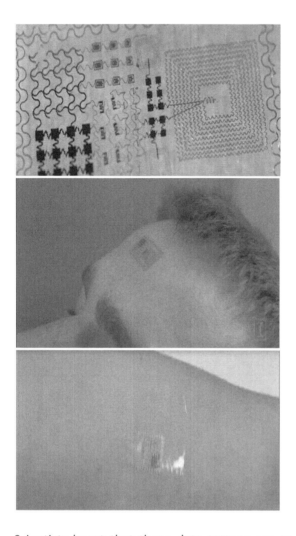

Scientists boast that these data tattoos are capable of flexing and bending with the movements of the skin with no loss of functionality. They can also be hidden underneath regular tattoos. This is something that has to be seen to be believed so you can find the report at http://www.youtube.com/watch?v=Dyk9Xnj4_5U. Dr Todd Coleman also recently gave a TEDx lecture in San Diego, CA explaining how doctors thought such data tattoos could be used to save newborn lives.[6]

"But humans will never submit to this invasion of privacy! People will never agree to be stamped with a number like a commodity and to have all their personal data held electronically. They'll never allow themselves to be trackable at all times by GPS!" That's another argument.

But the thing is...we're already halfway there.

For years now, our sense of privacy has been diminishing. On the one hand politicians have fed us the idea that if we want the state to keep us safe from terrorism and crime, we have to be willing to give up our privacy. We've gone along with it and are now tracked constantly, CCTV is everywhere, our number plates are scanned as we drive on the roads, we have emails intercepted, phone calls tapped and ID cards in our purses and wallets. We can't get on a plane without going through full body scanners. All the while we're spun the same old line that if we're innocent we have nothing to worry about. Oh, except loss of privacy...but that's not important...it's a necessary sacrifice...a price worth paying. So they say.

On the other hand, we increasingly give up our privacy *willingly* because our ever more technologically integrated lives demands it. Take social networking sites like Facebook and Twitter for example. People will now post every detail of their lives online for their friends, and sometimes all the world, to see. We share what we're having for dinner, what book we're reading, what movie we just saw, what item we just purchased, what school we went to, where we grew up, what our employment history is... even 'checking-in' to let our friends know where we are at an exact moment. Various companies vacuum this information up to create a profile of who you are for commercial gain. The more they know about you, the more they can tailor adverts for you. As social networking sites, and others, have developed new features, it has also become increasingly necessary to demolish old ideas of privacy to make them work.

Take Google for example. In mid 2012 they released a personal assistant for smartphones called Google Now. The idea behind it is that by monitoring your emails, your location data, your Google searches, likes and dislikes, it can present useful information to you before you even ask for it. Are you going to church on Sunday? Google already knows you are because it has been tracking your movements for several weeks and has noticed that you go there every Sunday morning. Therefore, when you wake up, it will automatically present you with traffic information and suggest the best route for getting to church that day. Are you catching a flight tomorrow? Google already knows you are because it mined your search data and emails, including the one the airline sent to confirm your reservation. Therefore, it will automatically tell you if the flight is on time and will present useful information about your destination. Quite simply, these benefits are fantastic and because they are fantastic, the privacy concerns are ultimately cast aside. Sure we'll let Google know everything about us, because they're giving us such great features in return.

That's not to say we don't feel slightly uneasy about what we're doing. With each new abolition of privacy, there is generally a small flurry of protest from users. A tiny percentage may even deactivate their Facebook account or use another search engine. But ultimately the majority reluctantly agree. And when they begin to enjoy the benefits of the services, they settle down to a slightly less private life, wondering why they ever felt so uncomfortable about it. Indeed, it's fair to say that whenever the perceived benefits of services outweigh privacy concerns, it won't be long before those privacy concerns are forgotten.

Facebook founder, Mark Zuckerberg, said as far back as 2010 that privacy was no longer a social norm. He said, *"People have really gotten comfortable not only sharing more information and different kinds, but more openly and with more people,"* he said. *"That social norm is just something that has evolved over time."*[7]

The social norm is changing. The younger generations and the generations to come will grow up having never known a time before Facebook, Google or the internet and so their esteem for privacy will already be highly diminished. You could even level that accusation at people today. As such, it will be increasingly easy to convince people of the benefits of a data tattoo that can communicate with the world around them. Especially if you need one to pay bills or get a job.

Believers in Christ will be the only ones who will reject this move. They will understand that to take this mark, to become a part of this economy, to become a part of this society, to worship this beast and submit to his rulership and authority as a Messiah under a one world government, is to reject Jesus Christ. They will understand that to do so is a betrayal that will lead to terrible judgement. Therefore, believers left on earth at this time will refuse it and either live as outcasts or face death for their treason. In the meantime, Christians must stand against the development of the one world order which is happening even now.

# THE ISLAMIC MESSIAH AND PROPHET

So we've now got a reasonable idea of how the Antichrist and False Prophet will work together to dominate the end-time empire. And what's very interesting is that currently almost *all* the world's religions are currently waiting for a Messiah.

Buddhists are waiting for one called Maitreya. Taoists are waiting for one called Li Hong. A mixture of Chinese Buddhism and Taoism waits for a Messiah called "Prince Moonlight". Hindus wait for the tenth and final Avatar called Kalki. Interestingly, he is known as "The Destroyer"(Abaddon in Hebrew). However, they believe this name is a good thing...in their eyes he will be the destroyer darkness, ignorance and confusion. In Zoroastrianism, they wait for Saoshyant, who they refer to as "The Man of Peace". They claim he will battle the forces of evil and ultimately succeed. In Rastafarianism, they believe Haile Selassie was the Christ, and that he will return in the future. New Agers, Theosophists and occultists are waiting for a world-unifying Christ too, as evidenced in the writings of Alice A Bailey and Madame Blavatsky.[8]

Since all the world's religions are waiting for a Messiah, if a ruler were to come along in the style that the Antichrist does, calling himself the Christ, presenting himself initially as a man of peace, performing miracles to support his claims, creating unity on the earth as the most talented, charismatic, eloquent and dominant figure in a one world system, you can see how the world would rally behind him. The people would celebrate his arrival. Each religion seeing in him their promised Messiah. There's an ecumenical movement at work even now, preparing the minds of the world for a global spiritual union. And this homogenisation of the world is creating the necessary conditions for the false Messiah.

The most interesting take on events perhaps comes from within Muslim eschatology though. As we've already noted, Muslims are waiting for a Messiah called the Mahdi, which means "The Guided One". They believe he will be a descendent of Muhammad who will become visible on earth exactly seven years before the "Day of Resurrection". They believe he will unite the Muslims under a global caliphate that destroys world nations and dominates the world. What's even more interesting is they believe the Mahdi will come back *alongside* Jesus Christ and *together* they will rid the world of error, injustice and tyranny....oh yes...and Christians and Jews. So Muslims are waiting for a double-act.[2] The Muslim similarities with the two beasts don't end there either.

In their book, "The Awaited Saviour", Muslim scholars Ayatullah Baqir al-Sadr and Ayatullah Murtada Mutahhari describe the Mahdi as being universal and belonging to the whole world:

*"A figure more legendary than that of the Mahdi, the Awaited Saviour, has not been seen in the history of mankind. The threads of the world events have woven many a fine design in human life but the pattern of the Mahdi stands high above every other pattern. He has been the vision of the visionaries in history. He has been the dream of all the dreamers of the world. For the ultimate salvation of mankind he is the Pole Star of hope on which the gaze of humanity is fixed... In this quest for the truth about the Mahdi there is no distinction of any caste, creed, or country. The quest is universal, exactly in the same way as the Mahdi himself is universal. He stands resplendent high above*

the narrow walls in which humanity is cut up and divided. He belongs to everybody. For all that and much more, what exactly is the Mahdi? Surely that is the big question which the thinking people all over the world would like to ask."[9]

So they believe that he will unite *all* the religious factions and bring the whole world together under a spiritual One World Order:

"The Mahdi will establish right and justice in the world and eliminate evil and corruption. He will fight against the enemies of the Muslims who would be victorious."[10]

"He will reappear on the appointed day, and then he will fight against the forces of evil, lead a world revolution and set up a new world order based on justice, righteousness and virtue...ultimately the righteous will take the world administration in their hands and Islam will be victorious over all the religions."[11]

They claim he will establish Islam on the entire earth, firstly by forming a caliphate/empire in the Islamic world and then waging a series of jihads (holy wars):

"al-Mahdi will receive a pledge of allegiance as a caliph for Muslims. He will lead Muslims in many battles of jihad. His reign will be a caliphate that follows the guidance of the Prophet. Many battles will ensue between Muslims and the disbelievers during the Mahdi's reign..."[12]

They believe that in order to prepare the way for the Mahdi, there will be a huge war where armies, originating in Iran, will go out to attack the world under the banner of black flags. They particularly believe that the West will suffer during this time. Sheikh Kabbani wrote:

*"Hadith indicate that black flags coming from the area of Khorasan will signify the appearance of the Mahdi is nigh. Khorasan is in todays Iran, and some scholars have said that this hadith means when the black flags appear from Central Asia, i.e. in the direction of Khorasan, then the appearance of the Mahdi is imminent."*[13]

The black flag in Islam is the flag of jihad. Next time you see a report on the news of an Islamic mob, look in the background and you'll normally always see what Sheikh Kabbani is describing. But when Muslims around the world see these black flags being raised in Iran at the right time, they are to unite under them wherever they live. Remember it would only take 12.5% of the world's Muslims to create the 200 million strong army.

*"The Messenger of Allah said: The black banners will come from the East and their hearts will be as firm as iron. Whoever hears of them should join them and give allegiance, even if it means crawling across snow."*[14]

Firstly, notice that this hadith compares their hearts to iron. Didn't Daniel describe the end-time empire as an empire of iron?

It also tells us that Muslims will come even from snow covered lands - in other words, the extremities of the earth - to join the army. This could well be the 200 million strong gathering that leads to a third of the world being killed; the event that signals the unveiling of the true nature of the Antichrist. And all this explains why Iran is so keen to launch a war on the world. They are *Khorasan,* and thus, they recognise that they have a central role to play in the return of the Mahdi. They think that by co-ordinating this attack, they will hasten his coming.

Indeed, since 2004, there has been an annual gathering in Iran called *"The International Conference of Mahdi Doctrine"* organised by the The Bright Future Institute. Their aim is *"to increase the knowledge about [Mahdi] both in Iran and abroad by supporting research and cultural works of other scholars."*[15]

Notably, Muslims also believe that the Mahdi will lead them to conquer Israel. At which point, he will establish Jerusalem as his base of power:

*"Rasulullah [Muhammad] said: "Armies carrying black flags will come from Khurasan. No power will be able to stop them and they will finally reach Eela (Baitul Maqdas in Jerusalem) where they will erect their flags."*[16]

*"Baitul Maqdas"* is Arabic for "the holy house". This is a reference to the structure on Temple Mount in Jerusalem - currently a Mosque, but soon to be a Temple again. Muslims believer the invading army will erect their black flags on Temple Mount to show their domination and ownership.

Egyptian author, Muhammad ibn Izzat and Muhammd 'Arif gives more insight into how they see this playing out:

*"The Mahdi will be victorious and eradicate those pigs and dogs and the idols of this time so that there will once more be a caliphate based on prophethood as the hadith states... Jerusalem will be the location of the rightly guided*

*caliphate and the center of Islamic rule, which will be headed by Imam al-Mahdi... That will abolish the leadership of the Jews... and put an end to the domination of the Satans who spit evil into people and cause corruption in the earth, making them slaves of false idols and ruling the world by laws other than the Shari'a [Islamic Law] of the Lord of the worlds."[17]*

And then there is this hadith which I have already presented. It applies to the time of Jerusalem's destruction:

*"The Prophet said... The last hour would not come unless the Muslims will fight against the Jews and the Muslims would kill them until the Jews would hide themselves behind a stone or a tree and a stone or a tree would say: Muslim, or the servant of Allah, there is a Jew behind me; come and kill him..."[18]*

We can see how the description of the Muslim Messiah matches up very closely to the Biblical description of the beast. It's a complete inversion of the truth. And this all adds more weight to the idea that the 200 million strong army, who come out of the area around the Euphrates, mentioned at the fifth trumpet, will actually be Islamic.

Very simply, Muslims are actively moving towards a new global caliphate, they believe that caliphate will be held together and ruled by a Messiah whose profile closely matches that of the Antichrist, they are openly hostile towards the two covenant peoples of God (believing Israel and Christians), their own prophecies predict the destruction of those peoples, their own prophecies predict a conquering of the world, their own prophecies predict an attack on Jerusalem, they are openly hateful of God himself, they have a history of terrorism and they have the numbers to raise a 200 million strong army. All of the arrows are starting to point towards them.

# CHAPTER 8. THE LAST MONTHS BEGIN

## THE 144,000 GO HOME

*"Then I looked, and behold, on Mount Zion stood the Lamb, and with him 144,000 who had his name and his Father's name written on their foreheads. And I heard a voice from heaven like the roar of many waters and like the sound of loud thunder. The voice I heard was like the sound of harpists playing on their harps, and they were singing a new song before the throne and before the four living creatures and before the elders. No one could learn that song except the 144,000 who had been redeemed from the earth. It is these who have not defiled themselves with women, for they are virgins. It is these who follow the Lamb wherever he goes. These have been redeemed from mankind as firstfruits for God and the Lamb, and in their mouth no lie was found, for they are blameless." (Rev 14:1-5)*

In this passage we see that the 144,000 have been raptured or *'redeemed'* from the earth and are now in the throne room of heaven. This is confirmed by the presence of the four cherubim and the twenty-four elders. Since we know that the 144,000 were appointed to hide in the wilderness for the 1,260 days of Jacob's Trouble, we must now be at the end of that period. Which means we're now transitioning into the very last two and a half months of history.

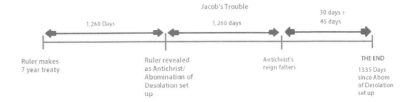

Remember that Daniel was told, *"From the time the daily sacrifice is stopped and the sacrilegious object that causes desecration is set up to be worshiped, there will be 1,290 days. And blessed are those who wait and remain until the end of the 1,335 days!" (Daniel 12:11-12)*

So after the 1,260 days of Jacob's Trouble, there will be another period of 30 days and then another period of 45 days beyond that. Two and a half months. We're now transitioning into that period.

Notice how the 144,000 are raptured as *"firstfruits for God and the Lamb."* Firstfruits is an agricultural term rooted in the Old Testament. To thank God for his provision, in early Spring each year (16th of Nisan on the Jewish calender), the people of Israel would take the first part of the grain harvest and offer it to him. This event was called the feast of firstfruits. So very simply, the firstfruits came to represent the first part of a much larger harvest.

In the New Testament, firstfruits took on a symbolic meaning that meant, 'a sign of what's to come'. For example, Paul refers to Epenetus as the firstfruits of the believers in Asia (Romans 16:5) while the household of Stephanas are referred to as the firstfruits of the believers in Greece (1 Cor 16:15). Paul's meaning is that they are the first to convert to Christianity in those regions but there will be a much larger harvest of souls to come after them.

Jesus Christ is also referred to as a type of firstfruits in the New Testament. Paul says, *"But in fact Christ has been raised from the dead, the firstfruits of those who have fallen asleep." (1 Cor 15:20)* Paul's meaning is that because Jesus has risen from the dead first, so will all those who belong to him. He is the sign of what's to come. The first of many. What's especially interesting about Jesus' resurrection is that it actually occurred on the 16th of Nisan...the Jewish feast of firstfruits! That was a prophetic sign. Because Jesus has been raised, so will all those who believe in him.

So the 144,000 being raptured to heaven as *"firstfruits for God and the Lamb"* at the seventh trumpet indicates to us that the general resurrection and rapture of *every* human being who has ever lived is now imminent. The larger harvest is on its way.

Now you may remember that I cast doubt on the idea that the church would be raptured at the sixth seal and here's why. If this rapture, which is only happening at the seventh trumpet, is the *firstfruits* rapture, then it suggests there have been no other raptures before this moment. And if that's the case, the noticeable shift in attention from the church to Israel back at the sixth seal seems more likely to be explained by martyrdom and apostasy than by a rapture. I'm still not willing to close the door completely on an earlier church rapture. Perhaps this *firstfruits* description only refers to the first rapture of the *Jewish* believers - after all it is their feast. But it's striking that when the church began filling up heaven at the sixth seal, they were explicitly described as martyrs in white robes, while, in contrast, there is no such mention of martyrdom or white robes for the 144,000. The implication seems to be that the church primarily leaves by martyrdom but these 144,000 have left by rapture. Must we therefore consider that a worldwide Christian holocaust in the future? Is that what will cause so many Christians to turn their backs on Christ, betraying their brothers and sisters in the process by turning them into the authorities? Or, can we still make a case for the church being raptured? I shall leave that one for you to ponder. (It may also be worth noting that during the Olivet Discourse, Jesus doesn't mention a rapture until *after* Jacob's Trouble either.)

Between the firstfruits harvest and the final harvest, God needs to use the intervening two and a half months to tie off all the loose ends on earth. And part of that means obliterating the Antichrist. His time is up. Returning to Isaiah's prophecy about the Assyrian, we read:

*"So this is what the Lord, the L*ORD *of Heaven's Armies, says: "O my people in Zion, do not be afraid of the Assyrians when they oppress you with rod and club as the Egyptians did long ago. In a little while my anger against you will end, and then my anger will rise up to destroy them." The L*ORD *of Heaven's Armies will lash them with his whip, as he did when Gideon triumphed over the Midianites at the rock of Oreb, or when the L*ORD'*s staff was raised to drown the Egyptian army in the sea." (Isaiah 10:24-26)*

The Antichrist thought he was destroying Israel by his own Satanic power and that no one could stand against him. What he didn't understand was that God was only allowing him to trample on Israel for seven years to conclude their punishment. His arrogance is unfounded. Ultimately God has always been in control. God says, *"the king of Assyria will not understand that he is my tool; his mind does not work that way. His plan is simply to destroy, to cut down nation after nation."* (Isaiah 10:7) However, now that God's anger against Israel has ended, he's going to turn the tables and destroy the Antichrist and his kingdom.

Who is left on earth during those very last two and a half months? Well, very few believers. Remember how Jesus said, " *when the Son of Man returns, how many will he find on the earth who have faith?"* (Luke 18:8) Clearly the inferred answer to his question is, "not many!" The church is pretty much gone and with the 144,000 raptured, all that's left are the believers who turned to God after seeing the two witnesses being resurrected in Jerusalem at the end of the 1,260 days. Those who I referred to earlier as the 11th hour converts. There may be others who responded to the Gospel as preached by the 144,000 or the two witnesses. We don't know for sure. Most of the believers will actually have been killed by the Antichrist by now. So the earth is almost totally devoid of true faith. Not quite. But almost. Almost everybody belongs to the Antichrist and his evil system. And the few believers who *are* left - these 11th hour converts - are actually very new, immature believers who have never been discipled. What is more, there's no chance of human discipleship now because the church and the 144,000 are gone. With no one to guide them through these last two and a half months, they're in a uniquely difficult situation.

To compensate for their lack of knowledge and for the general lack of a Christian presence on the earth, God now sends three angels to do supernaturally what is no longer possible naturally.

# THE THREE ANGELS

*"And I saw another angel flying through the sky, carrying the eternal Good News to proclaim to the people who belong to this world—to every nation, tribe, language, and people. "Fear God," he shouted. "Give glory to him. For the time has come when he will sit as judge. Worship him who made the heavens, the earth, the sea, and all the springs of water." (Rev 14:6-7)*

The preaching of the gospel *"to every nation, tribe, language, and people"* is a prophetic necessity that has to occur before the end. Jesus said, *"And the Good News about the Kingdom will be preached throughout the whole world, so that all nations will hear it; and then the end will come." (Matt 24:14)* So the end can't come until *everybody* has heard the gospel and had a chance to respond to it. That's only fair. And since there are no longer any mature believers on the earth to complete this task, it's necessary to send an angel instead. Presumably there are people in jungle tribes or people living in remote mountain villages who still haven't heard the gospel but this will be their chance. God keeps offering grace and mercy to everyone up until the *very* last moment. And with that loose end taken care of, there's now nothing left to stop the end from coming.

Indeed, the very reason that Jesus is delaying his return is to give everyone a longer chance to repent and accept the Gospel. Peter writes, *"The Lord isn't really being slow about his promise, as some people think. No, he is being patient for your sake. He does not want anyone to be destroyed, but wants everyone to repent." (2 Peter 3:9)*

God will be absolutely thorough and fair in giving the world *every* possible chance to be saved. When it's no longer possible naturally, he will even make it happen supernaturally. Some will take him up on the offer; others won't.

After the first angel has completed his preaching, God sends another. This one's job is to proclaim that Babylon is doomed.

*"Then another angel followed him through the sky, shouting, "Babylon is fallen—that great city is fallen—because she made all the nations of the world drink the wine of her passionate immorality.""* (Rev 14:8)

Prophetically, the word "Babylon" can be confusing. This is because it can represent a historical city, a religious system *or* a political system. Or a combination of all three!

You see, Babylon *was* once a literal city situated in modern-day Iraq. In Genesis 11, after the flood, many people congregated together there in defiance of God. They built a monument for their own glory which has become known as the tower of Babel. The tower of Babel was a political throne and an idolatrous temple - it had a political *and* religious significance. And the religion there was called The Mysteries. These were Satanic mysteries really. It involved the 'hidden secrets' of occultism and astrology. (Rev 2:24)

The Babylonian effort to co-ordinate a unified, God-defying, political and religious system was swiftly dealt with. Rather than destroying them with a flood, which is something he promised never to do again, God scattered them with different languages. However, as they spread out into the earth, forming different cultures, their religions retained elements of the Satanic

Mystery Babylon religion. Ever since that scattering, Satan has been trying to re-unify the earth under a global system once again - a one world order - in defiance of God. Babylon represents the origin and entirety of that evil system and ambition. It's a name that signifies the entire one world order led by the Antichrist.

So when the second angel shouts, *"Babylon is fallen—that great city is fallen"* we know it doesn't refer to the literal ancient city which actually fell long ago. It must represent the city in which the Antichrist's end-time empire is headquartered. The one that embodies this anti-God, Babylonian state of mind. The city which is the source and focal point of the global political tyranny *and* the worldwide false religion.

And that seems to point us in the direction of Jerusalem.

As far as we have been able to make out, Jerusalem is where the Antichrist will establish his throne. On Temple Mount. Earlier we had seen Jerusalem shockingly being referred to as Sodom and Egypt and we couldn't believe that God's Holy city could be described in such terms. It seems 'Babylon' here is just another horrifying code word for Jersualem in its current trampled, desolate state.

The role for the second angel is to warn the world that the Antichrist's global empire is about to fall and to turn to God before it's too late. The wicked people of the earth already killed the two witnesses for saying such things but the angel will now do supernaturally what's no longer possible naturally. The angel will tell them that although they consider the Antichrist to be unassailable and have put their faith in his system, his religion and his political structure, believing it to be invincible, it's about to be shattered by the true King. Jesus is coming back.

As Daniel wrote, *"During the reigns of those kings (10 end-time rulers), the God of heaven will set up a kingdom that will never be destroyed or conquered. It will crush all these kingdoms into nothingness, and it will stand forever."* (Daniel 2:44)

Anyone who puts their faith in the Antichrist is making a bad choice. Also notice how the angel talks about the fall of Babylon in the past tense. This is because it's as certain to happen as if it already *had* happened.

This angel may also be preaching to the few remaining baby believers too. Obviously, they won't have had a chance to read a Bible or have been taught about end-time prophecy from human beings, so this message from the angel will be vital information for them. It will help to orientate them with events at that time. You can imagine that they've just seen the two witnesses rising into heaven and know that God is God, but that's all they know. They don't have any clue about whether the Antichrist will continue to reign, how long for, what their stance should be if arrested, whether they are allowed to take his mark and participate in his system. They need this instruction. They need to know that Jesus' return is imminent and to hang on.

A third angel then comes along:

*"Then a third angel followed them, shouting, "Anyone who worships the beast and his statue or who accepts his mark on the forehead or on the hand must drink the wine of God's anger. It has been poured full strength into God's cup of wrath. And*

*they will be tormented with fire and burning sulphur in the presence of the holy angels and the Lamb. The smoke of their torment will rise forever and ever, and they will have no relief day or night, for they have worshiped the beast and his statue and have accepted the mark of his name."*

*This means that God's holy people must endure persecution patiently, obeying his commands and maintaining their faith in Jesus.*

*And I heard a voice from heaven saying, "Write this down: Blessed are those who die in the Lord from now on. Yes, says the Spirit, they are blessed indeed, for they will rest from their hard work; for their good deeds follow them!"(Rev 14:9-13)*

Again, this seems to be partly directed at the few baby believers on the earth. The 144,000 aren't there anymore to warn people against taking the mark of the beast so it's necessary for an angel to tell them supernaturally. And again, these few believers probably don't know about hell or the need to persevere through persecution so this is a mini sermon telling them what's required of them during the last two and a half months. They're being told *not* to take the mark of the beast; *not* to worship him in any way. Instead they must refuse and suffer whichever consequences come their way with patience and perseverance.

It seems that during this time, the screw will be turning on the Antichrist. His end won't come right away at the end of the 1,260 days; it's just that his power will start to weaken. He will no longer be able to do whatever he wants. As his empire starts crumbling during the last two and a half months, he will become increasingly desperate and will start assembling an army for

Armageddon - the climactic battle against God - and pressure will intensify to join his ranks. The Antichrist has wiped out most Christians, he's now trampled all over Israel and it will soon be time to confront God himself.

From a spiritual perspective, Satan lost the battle for heaven, but he still seems intent on claiming the earth as his through his stooge. This, in many senses, is the world's darkest hour - it's always darkest just before the dawn. Therefore, the three angels are sent to give everyone one last chance to repent and to offer a Discipleship 101 class to those new believers who are in the unfortunate position of still being around on earth at this time. Many of them will be martyred and those that aren't must be found to be faithful when the Lord returns for battle.

God pronounces a special blessing on these 11th hour converts for turning to him, and being willing to die for him, at such a dark time. And there's a part of us that perhaps may get a little riled by that. Why should these late-comers receive a special blessing? But in Matthew 20:1-16, Jesus tells a parable that explains how we have no right to be angry with God for being so merciful and gracious. Those who repent at the last minute will be treated just the same as those who converted 'earlier in the day.'

As for the rest of the stubborn people who are still refusing to turn to God, they have chosen their side and will soon suffer the consequences.

## THE HARVEST OF THE EARTH

*"Then I saw a white cloud, and seated on the cloud was someone like a son of man. He had a gold crown on his head and a sharp sickle in his hand.*

*Then another angel came from the Temple and shouted to the one sitting on the cloud, "Swing the sickle, for the time of harvest has come; the crop on earth is ripe." So the one sitting on the cloud swung his sickle over the earth, and the whole earth was harvested.*

*After that, another angel came from the Temple in heaven, and he also had a sharp sickle. Then another angel, who had power to destroy with fire, came from the altar. He shouted to the angel with the sharp sickle, "Swing your sickle now to gather the clusters of grapes from the vines of the earth, for they are ripe for judgment." So the angel swung his sickle over the earth and loaded the grapes into the great winepress of God's wrath. The grapes were trampled in the winepress outside the city, and blood flowed from the winepress in a stream about 180 miles long and as high as a horse's bridle." (Rev 14:14-20)*

This is more metaphorical imagery that gives a heavenly perspective on what's about to occur on earth. It's a preview. The firstfruits have already been raptured but now the whole earth is about to be harvested. In other words, those in Christ *and* those who have rejected him are *all* about to be removed.

The talk of a harvest connects us to Jesus' parable of the wheat and the weeds. He said, *"The Kingdom of Heaven is like a farmer who planted good seed in his field. But that night as the workers slept, his enemy came and planted weeds among the wheat, then slipped away. When the crop began to grow and produce grain, the weeds also grew.*

*"The farmer's workers went to him and said, 'Sir, the field where you planted that good seed is full of weeds! Where did they come from?'*

*"'An enemy has done this!' the farmer exclaimed.*

*"'Should we pull out the weeds?' they asked.*

*"'No,' he replied, 'you'll uproot the wheat if you do. Let both grow together until the harvest. Then I will tell the harvesters to sort out the weeds, tie them into bundles, and burn them, and to put the wheat in the barn.'" (Matthew 13:24-30)*

Jesus explains the meaning of the parable shortly afterwards saying that he will allow good and evil to coexist until the final harvest. Only after the harvest at the end of time will he separate the wheat from the weeds. The good will go into the barn which represents the house of God, while the evil will be burned up in hell. This is that harvest.

The talk of trampling grapes in *"the great winepress of God's wrath"* is a picture which specifically speaks of a violent and bloody destruction for the unbelievers. Obviously when grapes are trampled to make wine, the juice that flows out looks like blood. This vivid picture of blood flowing in a 180 mile long stream tells us that the massacre will be unparalleled.

How will all this come about? Through another set of seven plagues - this time, seven bowls. These seven plagues will culminate in Armageddon.

*"Then I saw in heaven another marvellous event of great significance. Seven angels were holding the seven last plagues,*

*which would bring God's wrath to completion. I saw before me what seemed to be a glass sea mixed with fire. And on it stood all the people who had been victorious over the beast and his statue and the number representing his name. They were all holding harps that God had given them. And they were singing the song of Moses, the servant of God, and the song of the Lamb:*

*"Great and marvelous are your works,*
  *O Lord God, the Almighty.*
*Just and true are your ways,*
  *O King of the nations.*
*Who will not fear you, Lord,*
  *and glorify your name?*
  *For you alone are holy.*
*All nations will come and worship before you,*
  *for your righteous deeds have been revealed."*
*(Rev 15:1-4)*

In the throne room of heaven, all those martyrs who were victorious over the beast during Jacob's Trouble are now in heaven standing on a sea of glass. This suggests they were part of the firstfruits resurrection and rapture. And if a tumultuous sea represents the wicked people of the earth, it seems that a sea of glass i.e. a perfectly calm one, represents a righteous people. They're totally at peace with themselves and with God.

Paul wrote to the Thessalonians about the seventh trumpet rapture when he said, *"And now, dear brothers and sisters, we want you to know what will happen to the believers who have died so you will not grieve like people who have no hope. For since we believe that Jesus died and was raised to life again, we also believe that when Jesus returns, God will bring back with him the believers who have died.*

*We tell you this directly from the Lord: We who are still living when the Lord returns will not meet him ahead of those who have died. For the Lord himself will come down from heaven with a commanding shout, with the voice of the archangel, and with the trumpet call of God. First, the Christians who have died will rise from their graves. Then, together with them, we who are still alive and remain on the earth will be caught up in the clouds to meet the Lord in the air. Then we will be with the Lord forever. So encourage each other with these words." (1 Thess 4:13-18)*

Paul is saying that the believers who have already died will be in heaven and will be right beside Jesus at the second coming. Notice that he also says it will happen "with the trumpet call of God." Which trumpet? Paul explains further to the Corinthians:

*"It will happen in a moment, in the blink of an eye, when the last trumpet is blown. For when the trumpet sounds, those who have died will be raised to live forever. And we who are living will also be transformed." (1 Cor 15:52)*

So the last trumpet, which is the seventh trumpet, which is where we now are in the timeline, is when all this will take place. All those who have died in Christ up until now will be taken up into heaven at this point, as will the church martyrs from the fifth seal, as will the 144,000, as will all those who were martyred during Jacob's Trouble. Here we see all of them assembling on the sea of glass in preparation for the triumphal return.

There will be some believers still alive on earth as we know and it seems some of them will manage to escape the clutches of the Antichrist and survive right up until the return of Christ. That's why Paul says that those who are still living at that point will not die, but will be transformed in the twinkling of an eye, rising to meet him (and us) in the air. That's why Daniel says, *"blessed are those who wait and remain until the end of the 1,335 days!"(Daniel 12:12)* Anyone who escapes the Antichrist's clutches right up until the very end will not taste death at all but will instead be transformed.

Here's the throne room picture to remind us of the general location of the sea of glass where they assemble.

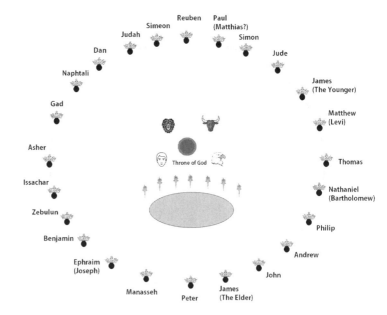

Before the final seven plagues, the believers in heaven break out into worship, in exactly the same way that there had been worship before the seals and trumpets.

*"Then I looked and saw that the Temple in heaven, God's Tabernacle, was thrown wide open. The seven angels who were holding the seven plagues came out of the Temple. They were clothed in spotless white linen with gold sashes across their chests. Then one of the four living beings handed each of the seven angels a gold bowl filled with the wrath of God, who lives forever and ever. The Temple was filled with smoke from God's glory and power. No one could enter the Temple until the seven angels had completed pouring out the seven plagues." (Rev 15:5-8)*

The time has come for God to complete his destruction by pouring out a final set of seven on the earth - this time seven bowls of wrath. The seven bowls of wrath come in rapid-fire succession over the final two and a half months of life on earth. They form part of the seventh and final trumpet of God. Here's an illustration to help place them:

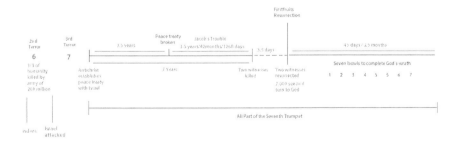

Seven angels are tasked with pouring out of the seven bowls - probably the same seven angels who blew the trumpets (the seven spirits of God represented by the flaming torches). The fact they are wearing their best clothes - white linen with gold sashes - portrays a feeling of dressing up for the main event. This is the day of redemption that all creation has been waiting for. John sees them entering the throne room of God and as they do so, one of the four cherubim - John doesn't specify which one - gives each one of them a bowl metaphorically containing the wrath of God.

The bowl metaphor is interesting. Remember when Jesus was praying in Gethsemane prior to his crucifixion and he said, *"My Father! If it is possible, let this cup of suffering be taken away from me. Yet I want your will to be done, not mine."* (Matt 26:39) Jesus refers to a cup because he is about to experience the cup of God's wrath against sin within his own frail human body. Likewise, God's culminating wrath against sin in the end-times is contained within these final seven bowls.

# CHAPTER 9. THE SEVEN BOWLS

## THE FIRST BOWL

*"Then I heard a mighty voice from the Temple say to the seven angels, "Go your ways and pour out on the earth the seven bowls containing God's wrath."*

*So the first angel left the Temple and poured out his bowl on the earth, and horrible, malignant sores broke out on everyone who had the mark of the beast and who worshiped his statue." (Rev 16:1-2)*

All those who had submitted to the rule of the Antichrist, who worshipped his statue and who took his mark, suddenly break out in horrible, malignant sores. God did a similar thing to the Egyptians before the Exodus and it will replicate that event.

Some have pointed out that there would be a certain poetic justice if the malignant sores were *caused* by the mark of the beast. God does employ poetic justice (see Matt 7:2)so this is certainly possible. Perhaps the microchip may react with the human body in such a way that it causes the sores. The word 'malignant' even puts us in mind of cancerous tumours. Interestingly, there are growing concerns that modern Wi-Fi signals and other types of radiation from items like mobile phones may be the cause of such tumours. If the mark of the beast contained similar technology and if it were tattooed or grafted onto the skin itself, it may cause this kind of reaction.

## THE SECOND BOWL

*"Then the second angel poured out his bowl on the sea, and it became like the blood of a corpse. And everything in the sea died." (Rev 16:3)*

Next, the whole sea turns to blood and is unable to sustain any life. Everything in the ocean dies. We've seen a third of the sea being affected in this way during the trumpets but here, the judgement is total. Obviously much of our food comes from the sea so this would be disastrous. However the third judgement is even worse.

## THE THIRD BOWL

*"Then the third angel poured out his bowl on the rivers and springs, and they became blood. And I heard the angel who had authority over all water saying,*

*"You are just, O Holy One, who is and who always was,*
*    because you have sent these judgments.*
*Since they shed the blood*
*    of your holy people and your prophets,*
*you have given them blood to drink.*
*    It is their just reward."*

*And I heard a voice from the altar, saying,*

*"Yes, O Lord God, the Almighty,*
*    your judgments are true and just.""  (Rev 16:4-7)*

All the natural sources of fresh water in the world becomes like blood. Again, we've seen part of the fresh water supply being cursed in the past but now the judgement affects the entire earth. You can imagine that without fresh drinking water, the people of the world start thirsting and dying from dehydration.

Indeed, since most people can only last about three days without water, there's only really one way in which they can survive...and that's to *drink* the blood!

Blood can essentially hydrate. Masai warriors in Kenya regularly drink blood mixed with milk. The Bible doesn't tell us that it's human blood they're drinking specifically, and the problem with human blood would be that it contains high levels of salt. However, even if it was human blood, the salt could be extracted. And interestingly,  big cats who have eaten humans are noticeable because they develop large, hairless sores on their skin because of that high salt content in the blood. Since the humans at this time will develop sores, does this mean they will, in fact, be reduced to cannibalism?

The angel who pours out this bowl notices some poetic justice again. He says that because these people had persecuted and spilled the innocent blood of God's people, gloating and celebrating their deaths like it was Christmas, it's only fitting that they have now been given nothing but blood to drink by God. It's like God is saying, "Blood-thirsty are you? Here, take your fill of the stuff."

## THE FOURTH BOWL

*"Then the fourth angel poured out his bowl on the sun, causing it to scorch everyone with its fire. Everyone was burned by this blast of heat, and they cursed the name of God, who had control over all these plagues. They did not repent of their sins and turn to God and give him glory." (Rev 16:8-9)*

The sun then blasts the people on the earth. We're either talking about a monstrous heatwave or something much worse. When allied to the fact that there is no fresh water to parch their thirst in the heat, you can imagine the terrible agony. However, these are people who are so hardened to God, that even now they don't repent. Instead, they curse him all the more.

## THE FIFTH BOWL

*"Then the fifth angel poured out his bowl on the throne of the beast, and his kingdom was plunged into darkness. His subjects ground their teeth in anguish, and they cursed the God of heaven for their pains and sores. But they did not repent of their evil deeds and turn to God." (Rev 16:10-11)*

The One World Order of the Antichrist is destroyed - his free reign over the earth only lasting 3.5 years. The world is plunged into darkness at this moment and those who submitted to him, now covered in sores and burns from the blast of heat from the sun, completely dehydrated and unable to find food from the rivers or oceans, find themselves in anguish. However, the Bible again points out that even now, they are *still* unrepentant!

## THE SIXTH BOWL

*""Then the sixth angel poured out his bowl on the great Euphrates River, and it dried up so that the kings from the east could march their armies toward the west without hindrance. And I saw three evil spirits that looked like frogs leap from the mouths of the dragon, the beast, and the false prophet. They are demonic spirits who work miracles and go out*

*to all the rulers of the world to gather them for battle against the Lord on that great judgment day of God the Almighty.*

*"Look, I will come as unexpectedly as a thief! Blessed are all who are watching for me, who keep their clothing ready so they will not have to walk around naked and ashamed."*

*And the demonic spirits gathered all the rulers and their armies to a place with the Hebrew name Armageddon." (Rev 16:12-16)*

When the sixth bowl is poured out, Satan, the Antichrist and the false prophet send out a call for all the nations of the world to gather together in defiance of God for a climactic battle. They gather in the valley of Megiddo, which is a vast plain in Israel, best viewed from the top of Mount Carmel. Notice that the frog like demons coming out of the dragon, Antichrist and false prophet, are really the ones orchestrating this gathering of defiance. This is why it's fair to believe that demons were also the ones behind the gathering of the 200 million back at the sixth trumpet. We're not told the significance of the frog-like appearance. But those armies who are demonically assembled come hoping to defeat God once and for all. In a sense, the torment of the previous bowls has forced their hand. They must make their stand against God now. However, they are spiritually blinded and don't understand that they are only gathering for their own destruction. They're about to be trampled in God's winepress.

Interestingly, we're told that the armies who come from the East will have to cross the Euphrates river, which is now dry. This is probably by virtue of the fact that, as a freshwater river, it has been turned to blood and then scorched by the heat of the sun during the previous bowls.

This final battle was also prophesied through Joel:

*"Say to the nations far and wide:*
*   "Get ready for war!*
*Call out your best warriors.*
*   Let all your fighting men advance for the attack.*
*Hammer your plowshares into swords*
*   and your pruning hooks into spears.*
*   Train even your weaklings to be warriors.*
*Come quickly, all you nations everywhere.*
*   Gather together in the valley."*
*And now, O LORD, call out your warriors!*
*"Let the nations be called to arms.*
*   Let them march to the valley of Jehoshaphat.*
*There I, the LORD, will sit*
*   to pronounce judgment on them all.*
*Swing the sickle,*
*   for the harvest is ripe.*
*Come, tread the grapes,*
*   for the winepress is full.*
*The storage vats are overflowing*
*   with the wickedness of these people."*
*Thousands upon thousands are waiting in the valley of decision.*
*   There the day of the LORD will soon arrive." (Joel 3:9-14)*

There we see the harvest reference again, highlighting the fact that this is when it will take place.

## THE SEVENTH BOWL

*"Then the seventh angel poured out his bowl into the air. And a mighty shout came from the throne in the Temple, saying, "It is*

*finished!" Then the thunder crashed and rolled, and lightning flashed. And a great earthquake struck—the worst since people were placed on the earth. The great city of Babylon split into three sections, and the cities of many nations fell into heaps of rubble. So God remembered all of Babylon's sins, and he made her drink the cup that was filled with the wine of his fierce wrath. And every island disappeared, and all the mountains were levelled. There was a terrible hailstorm, and hailstones weighing as much as seventy-five pounds fell from the sky onto the people below. They cursed God because of the terrible plague of the hailstorm."(Rev 16:17-21)*

Finally, the seventh bowl is poured out into the air and a great thunderstorm brews. As the thunder and lightning flashes across the sky, there is yet another huge earthquake - the worst earthquake in human history. It's so cataclysmic that the islands of the world disappear and the mountains are levelled. Furthermore, seventy-five pound hailstones fall from the sky. To give you an idea of what seventy-five pounds is, that's about the weight of a bag of concrete or about 100 cans of beer. Can you imagine the devastation of bags of concrete raining out of the sky?

The cities of the world collapse into ruins. No buildings can withstand that kind of siege. All our grand designs and monuments to greatness are brought to nothing. The Gentile cities are contrasted with 'the great city of Babylon' which will be split into three by the earthquake. There's that reference to Babylon again. And again, I suggest it means the city in which the Antichrist's global system of governance is headquartered - the home of Mystery Babylon encapsulated in the false religions and Satanic systems of the world. Jerusalem. Jerusalem is always described as 'the great city' which stands in contrast to the Gentile cities of the world. Indeed, Jerusalem has already been defined as 'the great city' in Revelation 11:8 when it was also being compared to Sodom and Egypt.

Even now, the godless people don't repent. Instead, they curse God all the more.

## THE GREAT PROSTITUTE

At this point there is an intermission while we are given greater insight into exactly how and why God will destroy 'the great city'. This city seems to matter more than anything to God. And that's further evidence that it probably means Jerusalem. Remember, Zechariah 2:8 tells us that Jerusalem is God's most precious possession.

*"One of the seven angels who had poured out the seven bowls came over and spoke to me. "Come with me," he said, "and I will show you the judgment that is going to come on the great prostitute, who rules over many waters. The kings of the world have committed adultery with her, and the people who belong to this world have been made drunk by the wine of her immorality."*

*So the angel took me in the Spirit into the wilderness. There I saw a woman sitting on a scarlet beast that had seven heads and ten horns, and blasphemies against God were written all over it. The woman wore purple and scarlet clothing and beautiful jewellery made of gold and precious gems and pearls. In her hand she held a gold goblet full of obscenities and the impurities of her immorality. A mysterious name was written on her forehead: "Babylon the Great, Mother of All Prostitutes and Obscenities in the World." I could see that she was drunk—drunk with the blood of God's holy people who were witnesses for Jesus. I stared at her in complete amazement.*

*"Why are you so amazed?" the angel asked. "I will tell you the mystery of this woman and of the beast with seven heads and ten horns on which she sits. The beast you saw was once alive but isn't now. And yet he will soon come up out of the bottomless pit and go to eternal destruction. And the people who belong to this world, whose names were not written in the Book of Life before the world was made, will be amazed at the reappearance of this beast who had died.*

*"This calls for a mind with understanding: The seven heads of the beast represent the seven hills where the woman rules. They also represent seven kings. Five kings have already fallen, the sixth now reigns, and the seventh is yet to come, but his reign will be brief.*

*"The scarlet beast that was, but is no longer, is the eighth king. He is like the other seven, and he, too, is headed for destruction. The ten horns of the beast are ten kings who have not yet risen to power. They will be appointed to their kingdoms for one brief moment to reign with the beast. They will all agree to give him their power and authority. Together they will go to war against the Lamb, but the Lamb will defeat them because he is Lord of all lords and King of all kings. And his called and chosen and faithful ones will be with him."*

*Then the angel said to me, "The waters where the prostitute is ruling represent masses of people of every nation and language. The scarlet beast and his ten horns all hate the prostitute. They will strip her naked, eat her flesh, and burn her remains with fire. For God has put a plan into their minds, a plan that will carry out his purposes. They will agree to give their authority to the scarlet beast, and so the words of God will be fulfilled. And this woman you saw in your vision represents the great city that rules over the kings of the world." (Rev 17:1-18)*

This is almost certainly the most difficult passage in Revelation to translate. Scholars have never managed to reach an agreement on what is going on here. So let's take it slowly.

We're presented with an image of a prostitute or harlot. Basically an unfaithful woman. Since a faithful woman always represents the bride of Christ and since the bride of Christ is made up of two covenant peoples - Israel and the church - a prostitute is one who rightly belongs to him but who has turned away to follow foreign gods or idols. If the church was still on earth at this time we would look for a false church and that would point us towards Rome, but since the church is gone and Revelation's focus has been increasingly narrowing on Israel and specifically Jerusalem, and since the text seems to be zeroing in on the destruction of a city figuratively called Babylon, we must once again entertain the idea that this prostitute is indeed Jerusalem.

There's a precedent for this. Through Isaiah God said, *"See how Jerusalem, once so faithful, has become a prostitute." (Isaiah 1:21)* Other cities are given the name. Nahum calls Nineveh a prostitute (Nahum 3:4) and Isaiah again, refers to Tyre as a prostitute (Isaiah 23:13-18), but none is so consistently referred to with this name than Jerusalem. Jeremiah calls Israel a prostitute (Jeremiah 3:6-10). Ezekiel does likewise (Ezekiel 16:15-22). Hosea does too (Hosea 4:12-13). All of them talk in the context of a people who made a vow of commitment to God but who broke those vows to follow other gods.

We are told that this prostitute *"rules over many waters"*. Many waters refers to the multitudes of people in the earth. So this is a city where the Antichrist has headquartered his global rule. That points us towards Jerusalem.

We're told that *"The kings of the world have committed adultery with her."* We know that the rulers of the world will defer ultimate authority to the Antichrist reigning in Jerusalem as part of a one world government. Indeed, this passage tells us, *"They (the ten rulers) will all agree to give him (the Antichrist) their power and authority."* It seems the adultery that has exasperated God's patience with Israel is their willingness to become part of the one world order in the first place. When the Antichrist comes along, Israel will put her faith for safety in the Antichrist's system rather than in God; Israel will make a peace treaty with the Antichrist for her future rather than by putting her faith in God. Remember Jesus said, *"I am come in my Father's name, and you receive me not: if another shall come in his own name, him you will receive." (John 5:43)(KJV)* Jesus seems to be saying, "when I, your true Messiah came glorifying God, you rejected me. But when the Antichrist comes glorifying himself, you accept him." That's the prostitution that causes God to unleash his wrath on the city for the final seven years. And when the Antichrist turns on Jerusalem (the prostitute) halfway into his reign, God will allow it to happen. He will only cut it short for the sake of his chosen ones.

We're then told that this woman is *"sitting on a scarlet beast that had seven heads and ten horns, and blasphemies against God were written all over it."* We already know that the beast with seven heads and ten horns is the Antichrist's end-time global empire. Again, that's who Israel has prostituted itself with.

Why is she wearing *"purple and scarlet clothing and beautiful jewellery made of gold and precious gems and pearls"*? The colour purple has throughout history, been a symbol of status and even royalty. Scarlet suggests wealth. As does the description of being adorned with precious jewellery. Jerusalem, as the centre of the end-time empire, is the centre of global wealth and commerce. This makes sense as it's from here that we saw the False Prophet implement his world economic system.

Why would she be the *"Mother of All Prostitutes and Obscenities in the World"*? As if being a prostitute isn't bad enough, she is the *source* of all prostitution and obscenities in the world! That's because she is the source of the false religion and the focal point of the Antichrist's one world government at this stage. She has become the new, figurative, Babylon. Furthermore, the obscenities taking place in this city under his reign will be the worst the world has ever seen. That's why Jesus had said that the time would have to be cut short just for the sake of his holy ones.

Why is she *"drunk with the blood of God's holy people who were witnesses for Jesus"*? Because under the Antichrist's rule, the people of God have been continuously persecuted and slaughtered there.

Why does John say that he *"stared at her in complete amazement"*? Because this is Jerusalem! This is supposed to be God's precious city. And it's completely under the control of his enemy, Satan. It's a shocking thing. However, that's what the prostitute metaphor is all about. It represents an entity that once had a right relationship with God but which doesn't now.

It says that *"The scarlet beast and his ten horns all hate the prostitute. They will strip her naked, eat her flesh, and burn her remains with fire."* Satan, the Antichrist, and his coalition of ten kings all actually hate Jerusalem. They hate it because it has always been the apple of God's eye. The attack on her refers back to the period of Jacob's Trouble.

## THE FALL OF BABYLON

The details of the destruction are then laid out for us:

*After all this I saw another angel come down from heaven with great authority, and the earth grew bright with his splendour. He gave a mighty shout:*

*"Babylon is fallen—that great city is fallen!*
*She has become a home for demons.*
*She is a hideout for every foul spirit,*
*a hideout for every foul vulture*
*and every foul and dreadful animal.*
*For all the nations have fallen*
*because of the wine of her passionate immorality.*
*The kings of the world*
*have committed adultery with her.*
*Because of her desires for extravagant luxury,*
*the merchants of the world have grown rich." (Rev 18:1-3)*

Jerusalem has become overridden with evil and is now the dwelling place of demons and foul spirits. This is why she must be destroyed.

*"Then I heard another voice calling from heaven,*

*"Come away from her, my people.*
*Do not take part in her sins,*
*or you will be punished with her.*
*For her sins are piled as high as heaven,*
*and God remembers her evil deeds.*
*Do to her as she has done to others.*
*Double her penalty for all her evil deeds.*
*She brewed a cup of terror for others,*
*so brew twice as much for her.*
*She glorified herself and lived in luxury,*
*so match it now with torment and sorrow.*
*She boasted in her heart,*
*'I am queen on my throne.*
*I am no helpless widow,*
*and I have no reason to mourn.'*
*Therefore, these plagues will overtake her in a single day—*
*death and mourning and famine.*
*She will be completely consumed by fire,*
*for the Lord God who judges her is mighty." (Rev 18:4-8)*

Notice how Jerusalem doesn't seem to be concerned that she has lost her relationship with God. She says, *I am no helpless widow, and I have no reason to mourn.'* It's almost like she has revelled in her divorce from God. So here God is warning his people to come out of her because he is obliterating her along with the Antichrist's world system.

"And the kings of the world who committed adultery with her and enjoyed her great luxury will mourn for her as they see the smoke rising from her charred remains. They will stand at a distance, terrified by her great torment. They will cry out,

"How terrible, how terrible for you,
   O Babylon, you great city!
In a single moment
   God's judgment came on you."

The merchants of the world will weep and mourn for her, for there is no one left to buy their goods. She bought great quantities of gold, silver, jewels, and pearls; fine linen, purple, silk, and scarlet cloth; things made of fragrant thyine wood, ivory goods, and objects made of expensive wood; and bronze, iron, and marble. She also bought cinnamon, spice, incense, myrrh, frankincense, wine, olive oil, fine flour, wheat, cattle, sheep, horses, chariots, and bodies—that is, human slaves.

"The fancy things you loved so much
   are gone," they cry.
"All your luxuries and splendour
   are gone forever,
   never to be yours again."

The merchants who became wealthy by selling her these things will stand at a distance, terrified by her great torment. They will weep and cry out,

"How terrible, how terrible for that great city!
   She was clothed in finest purple and scarlet linens,
   decked out with gold and precious stones and pearls!
In a single moment
   all the wealth of the city is gone!"

*And all the captains of the merchant ships and their passengers and sailors and crews will stand at a distance. They will cry out as they watch the smoke ascend, and they will say, "Where is there another city as great as this?" And they will weep and throw dust on their heads to show their grief. And they will cry out,*

*"How terrible, how terrible for that great city!*
*  The shipowners became wealthy*
*  by transporting her great wealth on the seas.*
*In a single moment it is all gone."*
*Rejoice over her fate, O heaven*
*  and people of God and apostles and prophets!*
*For at last God has judged her*
*  for your sakes." (Rev 18:9-20)*

These passages tell us that the Antichrist's capital city became the centre of the world's wealth generating power. It was the focus of global commerce. As such, it was the wealthiest city in the world. The mention of ship captains standing at a distance mourning her destruction is often misconstrued to mean "Babylon" is a port city, and therefore, that would rule out Jerusalem as a candidate. But the passage doesn't actually say that. It only says that all those who are involved in various branches of commerce and trade relied on that city and now "stand from a distance", distraught as they watch it burn.

Again, this makes sense if we understand that the False Prophet will establish his global economic system from Jerusalem. Once the city is brought down into rubble, the entire world's economy will go into meltdown.

*"Then a mighty angel picked up a boulder the size of a huge millstone. He threw it into the ocean and shouted,*

*"Just like this, the great city Babylon*
*will be thrown down with violence*
*and will never be found again.*
*The sound of harps, singers, flutes, and trumpets*
*will never be heard in you again.*
*No craftsmen and no trades*
*will ever be found in you again.*
*The sound of the mill*
*will never be heard in you again.*
*The light of a lamp*
*will never shine in you again.*
*The happy voices of brides and grooms*
*will never be heard in you again.*
*For your merchants were the greatest in the world,*
*and you deceived the nations with your sorceries.*
*In your streets flowed the blood of the prophets and of God's holy people*
*and the blood of people slaughtered all over the world." (Rev 18:21-24)*

The fact that the blood of the prophets and of God's holy people flowed through the streets of Jerusalem also seems to refer to Jacob's Trouble. But with great violence, the Lord will bring the Antichrist's system down to nothing. God's people rejoice about this in heaven.

## DOUBLE DESTRUCTION

Throughout our study there have been clues that have led us to believe the Antichrist will be Syrian and may even come from Damascus. Earlier on you may remember I said that although the Assyrian Empire covered those Euphrates nations of Turkey, Iraq and Iran, I believed that Syria would most likely be his birth place. The reason I said that was because of a prophecy that Isaiah gave. In Chapter 17 of his book, we read about a destruction of Jerusalem that seems to be linked to a simultaneous destruction of Damascus.

### A Message about Damascus and Israel

*This message came to me concerning Damascus:*

*"Look, the city of Damascus will disappear!*
*It will become a heap of ruins.*
*The towns of Aroer will be deserted.*
*Flocks will graze in the streets and lie down undisturbed,*
*with no one to chase them away.*
*The fortified towns of Israel will also be destroyed,*
*and the royal power of Damascus will end.*
*All that remains of Syria*
*will share the fate of Israel's departed glory,"*
*declares the LORD of Heaven's Armies.*
*"In that day Israel's glory will grow dim;*
*its robust body will waste away.*
*The whole land will look like a grainfield*
*after the harvesters have gathered the grain.*
*It will be desolate,*
*like the fields in the valley of Rephaim after the harvest.*
*Only a few of its people will be left,*
*like stray olives left on a tree after the harvest.*
*Only two or three remain in the highest branches,*

four or five scattered here and there on the limbs,"
  declares the LORD, the God of Israel.
Then at last the people will look to their Creator
  and turn their eyes to the Holy One of Israel.
They will no longer look to their idols for help
  or worship what their own hands have made.
They will never again bow down to their Asherah poles
  or worship at the pagan shrines they have built.
Their largest cities will be like a deserted forest,
  like the land the Hivites and Amorites abandoned
when the Israelites came here so long ago.
  It will be utterly desolate.
Why? Because you have turned from the God who can save you.
  You have forgotten the Rock who can hide you.
So you may plant the finest grapevines
  and import the most expensive seedlings.
They may sprout on the day you set them out;
  yes, they may blossom on the very morning you plant them,
but you will never pick any grapes from them.
  Your only harvest will be a load of grief and unrelieved pain.
Listen! The armies of many nations
  roar like the roaring of the sea.
Hear the thunder of the mighty forces
  as they rush forward like thundering waves.
But though they thunder like breakers on a beach,
  God will silence them, and they will run away.
They will flee like chaff scattered by the wind,
  like a tumbleweed whirling before a storm.
In the evening Israel waits in terror,
  but by dawn its enemies are dead.
This is the just reward of those who plunder us,
  a fitting end for those who destroy us."

*(Isaiah 17)*

This prophecy talks about a destruction of Damascus that coincides with a destruction of Israel. They have a "shared fate". It says that this will happen *"after the harvesters have gathered the grain"* and we have just been reading about the spiritual harvest of the earth. The harvesters are God's angels gathering the elect from the earth. This prophecy also says that the world's *"largest cities will be like a deserted forest"* and we have just been reading that the cities of the world will be ruined by seventy five pound hailstones. This prophecy also mentions the armies of the world coming together with a roar like the sea. This is something else that points us towards the gathering of the world's armies for Armageddon. This prophecy even mentions grapevines which vividly recalls God's "winepress" description of their destruction. We also read, *"Then at last the people will look to their Creator and turn their eyes to the Holy One of Israel"* so we know that this event will happen right before the second coming.

So while this unfulfilled prophecy from Isaiah was in the news a lot recently due to the civil war in Syria, and while many Christians speculated that we were about to witness the destruction of Damascus, I would suggest that this is a prophecy that won't find fulfilment until the time of the very end. It seems that the Antichrist's hometown may be destroyed in conjunction with the destruction of Jerusalem, his power base, and that's what the connection is.

## SONGS OF VICTORY IN HEAVEN

"After this, I heard what sounded like a vast crowd in heaven shouting,

"Praise the LORD!
   Salvation and glory and power belong to our God.
His judgments are true and just.
   He has punished the great prostitute
who corrupted the earth with her immorality.
   He has avenged the murder of his servants."

And again their voices rang out:

"Praise the LORD!
   The smoke from that city ascends forever and ever!"

Then the twenty-four elders and the four living beings fell down and worshiped God, who was sitting on the throne. They cried out, "Amen! Praise the LORD!"

And from the throne came a voice that said,

"Praise our God,
   all his servants,
all who fear him,
   from the least to the greatest."

Then I heard again what sounded like the shout of a vast crowd or the roar of mighty ocean waves or the crash of loud thunder:

"Praise the LORD!
   For the Lord our God, the Almighty, reigns.
Let us be glad and rejoice,
   and let us give honour to him.

*For the time has come for the wedding feast of the Lamb,
    and his bride has prepared herself.
She has been given the finest of pure white linen to wear."
    For the fine linen represents the good deeds of God's holy
people.*

*And the angel said to me, "Write this: Blessed are those who are
invited to the wedding feast of the Lamb." And he added, "These
are true words that come from God." (Rev 19:1-9)*

The countless numbers of believers in heaven are singing with
such joy and emotion about God's victory that John gets swept
up in the moment and forgets himself. He falls down to worship
the angel who was revealing all these things to him.

*"Then I fell down at his feet to worship him, but he said, "No,
don't worship me. I am a servant of God, just like you and your
brothers and sisters who testify about their faith in Jesus.
Worship only God. For the essence of prophecy is to give a clear
witness for Jesus." (Rev 19:10)*

He is swiftly corrected and told that no one should be
worshipped but God. He says that although he's the one
showing John the prophecy, its not intended to glorify himself.
Only to clearly testify to him the truth about Jesus.

Speaking of Jesus, it's finally time for him to come back to earth,
along with the believers who were part of harvest rapture, and
wipe out those enemies who have been strutting around the
world like they own the place.

## THE RETURN OF THE KING

*"Then I saw heaven opened, and a white horse was standing there. Its rider was named Faithful and True, for he judges fairly and wages a righteous war. His eyes were like flames of fire, and on his head were many crowns. A name was written on him that no one understood except himself. He wore a robe dipped in blood, and his title was the Word of God. The armies of heaven, dressed in the finest of pure white linen, followed him on white horses. From his mouth came a sharp sword to strike down the nations. He will rule them with an iron rod. He will release the fierce wrath of God, the Almighty, like juice flowing from a winepress. On his robe at his thigh was written this title: King of all kings and Lord of all lords.*

*Then I saw an angel standing in the sun, shouting to the vultures flying high in the sky: "Come! Gather together for the great banquet God has prepared. Come and eat the flesh of kings, generals, and strong warriors; of horses and their riders; and of all humanity, both free and slave, small and great."*

*Then I saw the beast and the kings of the world and their armies gathered together to fight against the one sitting on the horse and his army. And the beast was captured, and with him the false prophet who did mighty miracles on behalf of the beast— miracles that deceived all who had accepted the mark of the beast and who worshiped his statue. Both the beast and his false prophet were thrown alive into the fiery lake of burning sulphur. Their entire army was killed by the sharp sword that came from the mouth of the one riding the white horse. And the vultures all gorged themselves on the dead bodies." (Rev 19-11:21)*

Finally, the King is back. Finally! I get a rush of excitement just reading these words. It's the moment that all creation has been waiting for. This time Jesus arrives, not as a child, meek and mild, born in a manger, but as a mighty warrior, dressed for battle. He's back as a lion rather than a lamb. On his head are many crowns because he is not just the king - He's the King of kings. He's not just the lord - He's the Lord of all lords. His title is the Word of God. The armies of the world who dared to defy him by gathering together for Armageddon don't stand a chance. They are utterly annihilated. These hard hearted, unrepentant fools who rejected countless opportunities to repent and be saved are now, from the least to the greatest, left strewn across the valley of Megiddo. The birds of the air come down to feast on the dead flesh.

If you've come to believe that Jesus is a harmless pacifist you may be shocked by this side of his character. Yes, he is the Lamb of God, but he's also the Lion of the tribe of Judah. Indeed, *"The LORD is a warrior; The LORD is his name!" (Exodus 15:3)* And when the time comes, he will crush his enemies. In the process, the leaders of the rebellion - Satan's two puppets - the Antichrist and false prophet, will be captured and *"thrown alive into the fiery lake of burning sulphur."*

Imagine the scene of devastation on a planet that already resembles a wasteland from the battering it has taken over the preceding years. Seven seals, seven trumpets and seven bowls of wrath later, now the landscape is littered with dead bodies. Satan is captured too but isn't thrown into the lake of fire just yet:

*"Then I saw an angel coming down from heaven with the key to the bottomless pit and a heavy chain in his hand. He seized the dragon—that old serpent, who is the devil, Satan—and bound him in chains for a thousand years. The angel threw him into the*

*bottomless pit, which he then shut and locked so Satan could not deceive the nations anymore until the thousand years were finished. Afterward he must be released for a little while." (Rev 20:1-3)*

The angel coming down here with the key in his hand is probably the same one who came down to release Abaddon and his hoard of evil spirits during the fifth trumpet. He comes down to grab Satan and throw him into the bottomless pit for a 1000 year prison stretch. This 1000 year period is ruled by Christ and his bride.

*"Then I saw thrones, and the people sitting on them had been given the authority to judge. And I saw the souls of those who had been beheaded for their testimony about Jesus and for proclaiming the word of God. They had not worshiped the beast or his statue, nor accepted his mark on their foreheads or their hands. They all came to life again, and they reigned with Christ for a thousand years.*

*This is the first resurrection. (The rest of the dead did not come back to life until the thousand years had ended.) Blessed and holy are those who share in the first resurrection. For them the second death holds no power, but they will be priests of God and of Christ and will reign with him a thousand years." (Rev 20:4-6)*

Earlier we saw that Jesus had been given authority to open the seals, read the scroll and judge the world because he had remained faithful throughout his life on earth, even to the point of death on a cross. Here we see that Jesus willingly delegates some of that authority to those who faithfully followed after him - those who remained faithful even to the point of death. As Paul wrote to Timothy, *"If we endure hardship, we will reign with him. If we deny him, he will deny us."* (2 Tim 2:12) And as Jesus had already promised the church, *"To all who are victorious, who obey me to the very end, To them I will give authority over all the nations. They will rule the nations with an iron rod and smash them like clay pots."* *(Rev 2:26-27)* So although the focus of the first resurrection here is those who were beheaded during Jacob's Trouble (this is another very clear mark of Islam), when we take the wide angle view, we discover that the whole bride of Christ will share in the first resurrection and will help him rule over the world for a thousand years.

This thousand year period is often just referred to as "The Millennium" by Christians. Some try to spiritualise it and others claim it won't literally be a thousand years but in keeping with the KIS (Keep It Simple) approach, if the Bible explicitly says it's a thousand years, then we really shouldn't have any cause to doubt it.

In many senses we are all princes and princesses in training for that period of rule. And God is monitoring our progress. Jesus said, *"If you are faithful in little things, you will be faithful in large ones. But if you are dishonest in little things, you won't be honest with greater responsibilities. And if you are untrustworthy about worldly wealth, who will trust you with the true riches of heaven? And if you are not faithful with other people's things, why should you be trusted with things of your own?"(Luke 16:10-12)* God wants to see how you handle little responsibilities because he knows if you're faithful with those right now, he can entrust you to be faithful with much larger responsibilities when it comes to ruling the earth in the future.

Your little acts of kindness, generosity and honesty are not going unnoticed.

It's also important to notice that the world still won't be at peace during the Millennium so you won't have a complete life of ease. The Bible says that Jesus and his bride will have to rule with an iron rod and occasionally have to smash nations like clay pots. That suggests there will still be some who are opposed to Jesus' (and as co-heirs, our) authority. This is confirmed when we see what happens when Satan is released from his prison cell:

*"When the thousand years come to an end, Satan will be let out of his prison. He will go out to deceive the nations—called Gog and Magog—in every corner of the earth. He will gather them together for battle—a mighty army, as numberless as sand along the seashore. And I saw them as they went up on the broad plain of the earth and surrounded God's people and the beloved city. But fire from heaven came down on the attacking armies and consumed them.*

*Then the devil, who had deceived them, was thrown into the fiery lake of burning sulphur, joining the beast and the false prophet. There they will be tormented day and night forever and ever." (Rev 20:7-10)*

Upon his release from prison Satan tries to gather an army for yet another onslaught on Jerusalem, which has now been placed back in the hands of Jesus Christ. It is *"the beloved city"* again. The surprising thing is that the deception works *again*! Before the beginning of time Satan deceived a third of the angels into following him and they fell. He then deceived Adam and Eve into rejecting God and they did. Even after a thousand years in jail, he still hasn't lost his knack for deception, and human beings still haven't lost the knack for being deceived! However, his defeat with his newly assembled army is so swift that he shouldn't have bothered. Satan is thrown into the lake of fire where the Antichrist and false prophet already are, and they are tormented forever.[1]

## THE FINAL JUDGEMENT

*"And I saw a great white throne and the one sitting on it. The earth and sky fled from his presence, but they found no place to hide. I saw the dead, both great and small, standing before God's throne. And the books were opened, including the Book of Life. And the dead were judged according to what they had done, as recorded in the books. The sea gave up its dead, and death and the grave gave up their dead. And all were judged according to their deeds. Then death and the grave were thrown into the lake of fire. This lake of fire is the second death. And anyone whose name was not found recorded in the Book of Life was thrown into the lake of fire." (Rev 20:11-15)*

After the thousand year reign and the defeat of Satan, we now reach the final "Great White Throne" judgement where all human beings from the beginning of time until the end are resurrected and brought before the throne of God. There, they are judged according to their deeds. Those who appear in the Lamb's Book of Life go on to eternal life. Those whose name isn't found in the Lamb's Book of Life are thrown into the lake of fire, where Satan, the Antichrist and false prophet have already been sent.

Notice that it says, *"death and the grave were thrown into the lake of fire"*. This means there will be no more death after this point for death itself has been destroyed.

# CHAPTER 10. A NEW DAWN

With the world judged, evil eliminated and death destroyed, it's now time to start again. This is really the first time that true peace breaks out. John tells us that the old battered earth has gone and a new cosmos and a new earth is created for those who belong to God:

*"Then I saw a new heaven and a new earth, for the old heaven and the old earth had disappeared. And the sea was also gone."* *(Rev 21:1)*

Many people talk as though believers will live in heaven for all eternity but that's not what Revelation says. Revelation tells us that after the Great White Throne judgement, there will be a new universe created for us, with a brand new earth. This new earth will be every bit as real as the current one.

I find it very interesting that it says there won't be a sea. Personally, I quite like the sea and would be disappointed if the new earth didn't have one! And that makes me cautious as I interpret this passage. After all, what we want is the truth, not what is most palatable for me. However, since the sea has consistently and figuratively represented the restlessness of the wicked and the godless people around the world throughout this book, I want to at least leave the door open for the idea that it means the same thing again here. God said through Isaiah, *"But those who still reject me are like the restless sea, which is never still but continually churns up mud and dirt."* *(Isaiah 57:20)* He also said, *"there is no peace for the wicked"* (Isaiah 48:22) I want to suggest that this image of a sea-less earth just means that there won't be any godless or wicked people there. Instead, because of the pervading righteousness, it will be a place of calm and peace.

The centrepiece of the new earth is a new Jerusalem, just as the centrepiece of the old earth had been the old Jerusalem.

*"And I saw the holy city, the new Jerusalem, coming down from God out of heaven like a bride beautifully dressed for her husband.*

*I heard a loud shout from the throne, saying, "Look, God's home is now among his people! He will live with them, and they will be his people. God himself will be with them. He will wipe every tear from their eyes, and there will be no more death or sorrow or crying or pain. All these things are gone forever."(Rev 21:1-4)*

The new Jerusalem is no prostitute. She is like a beautifully dressed bride. And life in this new city reminds us of how it was in the Garden of Eden. God and man in close fellowship once more. Consequently, there will be no more death, sorrow, crying or pain. That's all gone forever. We can't really conceive of something so wonderful from here but it sounds amazing!

*"And the one sitting on the throne said, "Look, I am making everything new!" And then he said to me, "Write this down, for what I tell you is trustworthy and true." And he also said, "It is finished! I am the Alpha and the Omega—the Beginning and the End. To all who are thirsty I will give freely from the springs of the water of life. All who are victorious will inherit all these blessings, and I will be their God, and they will be my children.*

*"But cowards, unbelievers, the corrupt, murderers, the immoral, those who practice witchcraft, idol worshipers, and all liars—*

*their fate is in the fiery lake of burning sulphur. This is the second death." (Rev 21:5-8)*

Anyone who is faithful until the end will inherit this new life on the new earth. But notice how it says cowards will not inherit it. This means that anyone who betrays Christ in the face of the outward pressure from the world will forfeit their salvation. We are to endure all things and in doing so, we will be considered victorious on the final day. *"For God has not given us a spirit of fear and timidity, but of power, love, and self-discipline." (2 Tim 1:7)*

*"Then one of the seven angels who held the seven bowls containing the seven last plagues came and said to me, "Come with me! I will show you the bride, the wife of the Lamb."*

*So he took me in the Spirit to a great, high mountain, and he showed me the holy city, Jerusalem, descending out of heaven from God. It shone with the glory of God and sparkled like a precious stone—like jasper as clear as crystal. The city wall was broad and high, with twelve gates guarded by twelve angels. And the names of the twelve tribes of Israel were written on the gates. There were three gates on each side—east, north, south, and west. The wall of the city had twelve foundation stones, and on them were written the names of the twelve apostles of the Lamb." (Rev 21:9-14)*

There's some excitement in this passage as the angel grabs John and says, *"Come with me!"* It's almost like he can't wait to show John the full widescreen, panoramic view of the glorious new Jerusalem. The angel takes him to a nearby mountain to get the best view as it's being put into place. Once more, John's vocabulary is stretched to breaking point as he tries to describe what he is witnessing. It sparkles and shines and reminds him of precious materials like jasper and crystal. It's awe-inspiring.

As we noted earlier, each of the twelve tribes of Israel will be honoured forever by having a gate named after them. Each of the twelve disciples will be similarly honoured by having a foundation stone inscribed with their name. The two covenant peoples of God, Israel and the church, recognised forever.

*"The angel who talked to me held in his hand a gold measuring stick to measure the city, its gates, and its wall. When he measured it, he found it was a square, as wide as it was long. In fact, its length and width and height were each 1,400 miles. Then he measured the walls and found them to be 216 feet thick (according to the human standard used by the angel)." (Rev 21:15-17)*

The size of the new Jerusalem is immense. 1,400 square miles is about the size of Indonesia. Also, notice that it's a cube shape. In the old Tabernacle, the place where God's presence resided was a cube shaped room called the Holy of Holies. In the future, the entire city will be God's dwelling place. The entire city will be the Holy of Holies.

*"The wall was made of jasper, and the city was pure gold, as clear as glass. The wall of the city was built on foundation stones inlaid with twelve precious stones: the first was jasper, the second sapphire, the third agate, the fourth emerald, the fifth onyx, the sixth carnelian, the seventh chrysolite, the eighth beryl, the ninth topaz, the tenth chrysoprase, the eleventh jacinth, the twelfth amethyst.*

*The twelve gates were made of pearls—each gate from a single pearl! And the main street was pure gold, as clear as glass."(Rev 21:18-21)*

Each of the twelve foundation stones will not only be inscribed with a disciple's name, but each will also be inlaid with a precious jewel too. The Bible doesn't tell us which disciple gets which jewel and it doesn't really matter. It's just a lovely touch from God that shows how precious they are to him. It reminds us of a husband buying some jewellery for his bride.

The twelve tribes of Israel will be similarly honoured. Each of their gates will be constructed with pearl. They're going to look absolutely spectacular.

Pearl gates obviously brings to mind the phrase, "the pearly gates of heaven" which has entered into the lexicon of the general population. Because of an unfortunate Catholic influence, it brings to mind a cartoonish view of Peter standing outside a single gate with a giant key and a guest list. Beyond the gates is normally a land of clouds and harps. However, we would do well to eradicate this kind of thinking from our minds. There will be twelve pearl gates - not one - and they are the twelve entry points into a literal new city in a literal new planet earth in a literal new universe. Not some gateway into dreamy cloudyness.

*"I saw no temple in the city, for the Lord God Almighty and the Lamb are its temple. And the city has no need of sun or moon, for the glory of God illuminates the city, and the Lamb is its light. The nations will walk in its light, and the kings of the world will enter the city in all their glory. Its gates will never be closed at the end of day because there is no night there. And all the*

*nations will bring their glory and honour into the city. Nothing evil will be allowed to enter, nor anyone who practices shameful idolatry and dishonesty—but only those whose names are written in the Lamb's Book of Life."(Rev 21:22-27)*

So the new city won't need a temple. In reality, we haven't needed a temple since Jesus' first coming. But now God and His Son will walk amongst the men and women and live with them. Imagine seeing Jesus on your way to the park and stopping for a chat in the street! That's the kind of picture that Revelation paints. The King of kings will dwell with his people and mingle with them freely.

This passage almost makes it clear that a world will exist outside the city. Revelation has a strong focus on Jerusalem and we know that's because it's the most important possession of God, but the world outside it will be every bit as diverse, if not more so, than the one we know today. Jerusalem will remain the centre of the world, just as it is today, but there will be other continents and landscapes and nations outside of it, just like today. The Bible says that the nations of the new earth will each have kings too.

It's often been wondered why the city would need walls and gates at all since these were historically built for security. Especially ones that are 216 feet thick! Does their presence suggest that the nations outside Jerusalem will pose a threat to the city? Not at all. In fact, whereas city gates throughout history were always closed each night for security, we are told here that the new Jerusalem's gates will never be closed. In other words, the gates and walls are only aesthetic! They have no military purpose. The nations of the new world will only bring honour and glory into the new Jerusalem.

What's emerging here is a picture of a city which is bustling with activity as people come and go from the nations. The kings of the other nations are most likely those believers who showed themselves to be trustworthy with little things here on earth, and so have now been entrusted with much there. You might be one of them. I suspect that even those who live outside the New Jerusalem will have a home there and will visit frequently. So there will be a lot of coming and going and much vibrancy on the streets of that cosmopolitan city.

Another key point is that the city of Jerusalem won't have any need of a sun or moon because it will be filled with the light of the Lord. As this light is continuous, it will never get dark. It should be noted that this description is specific to the city only. The rest of the world may well continue to go through night and day cycles. We don't know.

*"Then the angel showed me a river with the water of life, clear as crystal, flowing from the throne of God and of the Lamb. It flowed down the centre of the main street. On each side of the river grew a tree of life, bearing twelve crops of fruit, with a fresh crop each month. The leaves were used for medicine to heal the nations." (Rev 22:1-2)*

The main street in the new Jerusalem is going to be quite unlike anything you've ever seen. A river is going to flow down the centre from the throne of God and on either side of the banks, there will be two huge trees that will be capable of bearing twelve types of fruit. There will be a different type of fruit on the trees during each month of the year and the leaves of the trees will also have tremendous medicinal qualities. The medicines produced from these trees will keep the nations of the world in perfect health. Doctors are going to have an easy job on the new earth!

*"No longer will there be a curse upon anything. For the throne of God and of the Lamb will be there, and his servants will worship him. And they will see his face, and his name will be written on their foreheads. And there will be no night there—no need for lamps or sun—for the Lord God will shine on them. And they will reign forever and ever." (Rev 22:3-5)*

The curse that God placed on the earth back in Genesis has now been removed meaning people no longer have to toil to grow food. We're back to the days of Eden where food was ready for the picking, just hanging off the branches of the trees for free consumption. So yes, there will be food on the new earth. In fact, if you think you've tasted some good food here, wait till you try the food there! Everything on this earth has been affected by the curse of the fall. That means the fruit we eat, as good as it is, is a shadow of what it was originally designed to be. You'll never have eaten peaches as juicy as the peaches you'll eat on the new earth. You've never had a strawberry as packed with flavour as the ones you'll eat there. Not only that, but since our bodies are currently affected by the fall, including our tastebuds, we're not currently able to pick up the full range and depths of flavours that we could. We will there. On the new earth, our tastebuds will be perfectly tuned. So the food won't only be juicier, more flavoursome and more sweet, but we'll be better able to appreciate it.

## THE NEW EARTH WILL BE *MORE*

I think one of our problems is that we tend to think of the next life as being something *less* than this one.

When you think of the next life you probably think of something ethereal, dream-like, ghostly or intangible. That seems less appealing than this world which is real, tangible and touchable. When you think of the next life you probably think of something colourless and white. That seems far less appealing than this world which is just full of vibrant colour. When you think of the next world you probably think there are no animals or diversity of life. That seems far less appealing than this world which is full of fascinating species and pets who bring so much joy to our lives. When you think of the next world you probably imagine yourself to be in a kind of vegetative state, either plucking on a harp and staring serenely into the middle distance for all eternity or singing in a choir as part of never-ending church service. Frankly, that sounds truly awful. Far less appealing than this world which engages ours minds and which is full of discovery, new ideas, new hobbies, new skills, new foods, new places to explore and people to meet.

What I think we need to do is start realising that the next world will be *more*. More in every sense. It will be more tangible, more touchable, more delicious, more colourful, more diverse, more interesting, more discoverable, more spectacular and full of even greater friendships, joy, laughter and fun. You'll have a real body and you'll be able to do real things with it. You'll be able to play sports and build things. You'll be able to meet people for lunch and travel. You'll be able to go hiking and play video games and make music and read books. You'll be able to do these things with complete freedom. No bureaucracy, visas, permits, taxes or financial restrictions.

Because we have been given a cartoonish, and honestly not very appealing depiction of the new earth, Christians often aren't very excited about going. They've been robbed of their hope for the future. There's a feeling that since we all have to die and there are only two possible destinations, we'll take heaven because it's preferable to hell, but really, neither of them sound as interesting as earth. Playing a harp on a cloud for eternity...who would actually want that? With this in mind, Christians can scramble to escape death with all the fear and uncertainty of a non-Christian. Notice that non-Christians are constantly trying to reverse time, preserve youth, hide from death. It's their greatest enemy and ultimate fear. Christians *should* have a completely different attitude. To Christians, death is nothing. Absolutely nothing. It's just the front door that we have to walk through to enter our new life.

Jesus said, *"I am the resurrection and the life. Anyone who believes in me will live, even after dying. Everyone who lives in me and believes in me will never ever die." (John 11:25-26)*

Paul mocked death saying, *"Death is swallowed up in victory. O death, where is your victory? O death, where is your sting?" (1 Cor 15:55)*

It's nothing. For those who have eternal life, death is no real tragedy. Christians should stride confidently onwards knowing that each passing day brings us one step closer to something so much better than this. And it will be better. The new earth will be *more* in every sense.

Indeed, when Jesus said, *"...I am going to prepare a place for you...When everything is ready, I will come and get you, so that you will always be with me where I am." (John 14:2-3)* we mustn't think the place he is preparing will be anything less than stunning. We mustn't doubt his goodness. If you like this place, just wait until you see what he's got lined up for us next! Jesus is crafting something truly amazing.

I can also guarantee that although an endless worship service sounds terrible right now, we're going to be so happy to be there that worship, singing and dancing will come completely naturally. So yes, do expect to be doing a lot of those things. The parties of celebration on the new earth are going to be like nothing else you've ever experienced and worshipping God will be one of the best parts about being there! We should look forward with confidence to all these things.

## JESUS' MESSAGE

As Revelation begins to come to close, the angel tells John that everything he has seen is sure to happen:

*Then the angel said to me, "Everything you have heard and seen is trustworthy and true. The Lord God, who inspires his prophets, has sent his angel to tell his servants what will happen soon." (Rev 22:6)*

Jesus adds:

*"Look, I am coming soon! Blessed are those who obey the words of prophecy written in this book." (Re 21:7)*

John then confirms what his role has been in the production of the book:

*"I, John, am the one who heard and saw all these things. And when I heard and saw them, I fell down to worship at the feet of the angel who showed them to me. But he said, "No, don't worship me. I am a servant of God, just like you and your brothers the prophets, as well as all who obey what is written in this book. Worship only God!"*

*Then he instructed me, "Do not seal up the prophetic words in this book, for the time is near. Let the one who is doing harm continue to do harm; let the one who is vile continue to be vile; let the one who is righteous continue to live righteously; let the one who is holy continue to be holy."(Rev 21:8-11)*

The reason John is told not to seal up the book is because God wants us to hear it and understand it. Revelation has information that is relevant and pertinent for us today. Again, many people refuse to get involved with Revelation fearing the strange imagery or believing it to be unimportant for daily life. However, it's in the Bible because God wants us to read it and understand it and it benefits us to do both. Having this understanding will help us to deal with a difficult future, which is going to get a lot worse before it gets better.

Jesus adds another message to sign off the book personally:

*"Look, I am coming soon, bringing my reward with me to repay all people according to their deeds. I am the Alpha and the Omega, the First and the Last, the Beginning and the End."*

*Blessed are those who wash their robes. They will be permitted to enter through the gates of the city and eat the fruit from the tree of life. Outside the city are the dogs—the sorcerers, the* sexually immoral, the murderers, the idol worshipers, and all who love to live a lie."(Rev 22:12-15)

Note that "dogs" is not literal but is rather just a general derogatory term. A similar word would be "pigs". Also note that when it says these evil people will not be allowed to enter the new Jerusalem, that doesn't mean they're in the surrounding nations. It just confirms that they're all in hell, outer darkness, having been sent there during the Great White Throne Judgement. They will not have *any* part in the new creation.

*"I, Jesus, have sent my angel to give you this message for the churches. I am both the source of David and the heir to his throne. I am the bright morning star."*

*The Spirit and the bride say, "Come." Let anyone who hears this say, "Come." Let anyone who is thirsty come. Let anyone who desires drink freely from the water of life. And I solemnly declare to everyone who hears the words of prophecy written in this book: If anyone adds anything to what is written here, God will add to that person the plagues described in this book. And if anyone removes any of the words from this book of prophecy, God will remove that person's share in the tree of life and in the holy city that are described in this book.*

*He who is the faithful witness to all these things says, "Yes, I am coming soon!"*

*Amen! Come, Lord Jesus!*

*May the grace of the Lord Jesus be with God's holy people."* *(Revelation 22:16-21)*

This sign-off on Revelation shows how seriously Jesus takes this book. Anyone who adds or takes away from it will be cursed!

# CONCLUSION

The road ahead is painfully difficult for Christians. I hope this study has given an accurate account of just how painful it will be. But I hope it's also shown that the end will be worth it.

Jesus may never ask you to suffer and die for him. You may never have to become a martyr for his name. But he may. And if he does, don't be surprised or think that something unusual is happening. And know that a great reward awaits you on the other side.

Don't be sad to leave. What you'll wake up to will be more than you could ever dream or hope for. This world is a wilderness - a desert - compared to the beauty of the world to come. We're exiles here. Strangers. (1 Peter 2:11) We're like the Israelites who left Egypt and spent 40 years wandering, dreaming of the land of milk and honey. That land is up ahead for us. We were never meant to get comfortable here.

We should be like soldiers dreaming of home. Have you ever seen those war movies where a soldier is in a war zone, covered in dirt, sweat and blood. The landscape is war torn buildings, riddled with bullets and crumbling to the ground because of the mortar shells and missiles. The sound all around him is screaming, panic, and gunfire. The soldier finds a spot and takes a photograph out of his pocket...a photograph of his wife and family. He looks at it and in his imagination the guns fall silent as he drifts back to the peaceful American Midwest. To his loved ones. To golden fields of wheat underneath a clear blue sky and no sound but the gentle rustle of the crops swaying in the breeze. He longs to be there. He aches to go home. And then an explosion goes off and he's drawn back into the present war-torn reality of life on the front line. He grabs his gun and heads off into battle knowing that he must fulfil his duty before he leaves. That should be Christians. Dreaming of home. Aching for glory. But knowing that we must fulfil our duty on this ravaged, war-torn earth first.

Paul wrote, *"Yet what we suffer now is nothing compared to the glory he will reveal to us later." (Romans 8:18)* That's quite a bold claim to make when we consider the pain and suffering that many people go through every day. It's an even bolder claim to make when we consider the horrors that await Christians in the time to come. Yet Paul says that however bad that is, it's *nothing* compared to the glory of what will come later. It will all be worth it.

When the world is being overrun by evil and it seems like all is lost, don't lose heart. Even when you're being pressured to abandon your faith and go with the flow - to get involved in New Age religion or occultism or any other religion - and when you're being persecuted for being the only one to believe in Christ in the workplace or the school, don't give up. Don't stop trusting that this is all happening just as Jesus said it would and that after the night will come the morning. The darkest hour is always just before the sun rise. And don't stop carrying out your duties. Preach the gospel, shine a light into the darkness, be faithful in every small thing. You're training to be a king or a queen one day.

At the world's darkest hour, it's going to seem like Jesus is never coming back at all and that he's forgotten us. When the Antichrist is strutting around on the world stage subjugating believers, trampling over Israel and doing whatever he wants for three and a half years, it's going to seem unbearable. Three and a half years might be short in the context of human history but it's going to seem like an eternity for those who go through it. In the off-chance that this book survives until then and you're reading it in those days, just hang on. Your hope will be rewarded. A great blessing awaits you. In the words of the writer to the Hebrews:

"Think back on those early days when you first learned about Christ. Remember how you remained faithful even though it meant terrible suffering. Sometimes you were exposed to public ridicule and were beaten, and sometimes you helped others who were suffering the same things. You suffered along with those who were thrown into jail, and when all you owned was taken from you, you accepted it with joy. You knew there were better things waiting for you that will last forever.

So do not throw away this confident trust in the Lord. Remember the great reward it brings you! Patient endurance is what you need now, so that you will continue to do God's will. Then you will receive all that he has promised.

"For in just a little while,
    the Coming One will come and not delay.
And my righteous ones will live by faith.
    But I will take no pleasure in anyone who turns away."

But we are not like those who turn away from God to their own destruction. We are the faithful ones, whose souls will be saved." (Hebrews 10:32-39)

For all it's strange and brutal imagery, Revelation is ultimately a book of hope that honestly tells us that while there will be abject misery and turmoil for a while, it will all be worth it in the end. Do not abandon the faith. He is coming. Just hold on. It *will* all be worth it.

*Download the complete Revelation timeline at*
*thefuelproject.org*

# APPENDIX 1 - Revelation 1 , 2 & 3

For the purposes of this book, I wanted to focus on the future aspect of Revelation, namely chapters 4-22. However, when Jesus said that those who took away from the book would be under a curse, I take that very seriously. Therefore, I am including chapters 1-3 here as an Appendix, so that the entire book is represented. The version used here is the New Living Translation (NLT).

**REVELATION 1**

**Prologue**

**1** This is a revelation from Jesus Christ, which God gave him to show his servants the events that must soon take place. He sent an angel to present this revelation to his servant John, [2] who faithfully reported everything he saw. This is his report of the word of God and the testimony of Jesus Christ.

[3] God blesses the one who reads the words of this prophecy to the church, and he blesses all who listen to its message and obey what it says, for the time is near.

**John's Greeting to the Seven Churches**

[4] This letter is from John to the seven churches in the province of Asia.

Grace and peace to you from the one who is, who always was, and who is still to come; from the sevenfold Spirit before his throne; [5] and from Jesus Christ. He is the faithful witness to these things, the first to rise from the dead, and the ruler of all the kings of the world.

All glory to him who loves us and has freed us from our sins by shedding his blood for us. [6] He has made us a Kingdom of priests for God his Father. All glory and power to him forever and ever! Amen.

[7] Look! He comes with the clouds of heaven.
  And everyone will see him—
  even those who pierced him.
And all the nations of the world
  will mourn for him.
Yes! Amen!

[8] "I am the Alpha and the Omega—the beginning and the end," says the Lord God. "I am the one who is, who always was, and who is still to come—the Almighty One."

## Vision of the Son of Man

[9] I, John, am your brother and your partner in suffering and in God's Kingdom and in the patient endurance to which Jesus calls us. I was exiled to the island of Patmos for preaching the word of God and for my testimony about Jesus. [10] It was the Lord's Day, and I was worshiping in the Spirit. Suddenly, I heard behind me a loud voice like a trumpet blast. [11] It said, "Write in a book everything you see, and send it to the seven churches in the cities of Ephesus, Smyrna, Pergamum, Thyatira, Sardis, Philadelphia, and Laodicea."

[12] When I turned to see who was speaking to me, I saw seven gold lampstands. [13] And standing in the middle of the

lampstands was someone like the Son of Man. He was wearing a long robe with a gold sash across his chest. [14] His head and his hair were white like wool, as white as snow. And his eyes were like flames of fire. [15] His feet were like polished bronze refined in a furnace, and his voice thundered like mighty ocean waves. [16] He held seven stars in his right hand, and a sharp two-edged sword came from his mouth. And his face was like the sun in all its brilliance.

[17] When I saw him, I fell at his feet as if I were dead. But he laid his right hand on me and said, "Don't be afraid! I am the First and the Last. [18] I am the living one. I died, but look—I am alive forever and ever! And I hold the keys of death and the grave.

[19] "Write down what you have seen—both the things that are now happening and the things that will happen. [20] This is the meaning of the mystery of the seven stars you saw in my right hand and the seven gold lampstands: The seven stars are the angels of the seven churches, and the seven lampstands are the seven churches.

## REVELATION 2

### The Message to the Church in Ephesus

**2** "Write this letter to the angel of the church in Ephesus. This is the message from the one who holds the seven stars in his right hand, the one who walks among the seven gold lampstands:

[2] "I know all the things you do. I have seen your hard work and your patient endurance. I know you don't tolerate evil people. You have examined the claims of those who say they are

apostles but are not. You have discovered they are liars. [3] You have patiently suffered for me without quitting.

[4] "But I have this complaint against you. You don't love me or each other as you did at first![5] Look how far you have fallen! Turn back to me and do the works you did at first. If you don't repent, I will come and remove your lampstand from its place among the churches. [6] But this is in your favor: You hate the evil deeds of the Nicolaitans, just as I do.

[7] "Anyone with ears to hear must listen to the Spirit and understand what he is saying to the churches. To everyone who is victorious I will give fruit from the tree of life in the paradise of God.

## The Message to the Church in Smyrna

[8] "Write this letter to the angel of the church in Smyrna. This is the message from the one who is the First and the Last, who was dead but is now alive:

[9] "I know about your suffering and your poverty—but you are rich! I know the blasphemy of those opposing you. They say they are Jews, but they are not, because their synagogue belongs to Satan.[10] Don't be afraid of what you are about to suffer. The devil will throw some of you into prison to test you. You will suffer for ten days. But if you remain faithful even when facing death, I will give you the crown of life.

[11] "Anyone with ears to hear must listen to the Spirit and understand what he is saying to the churches. Whoever is victorious will not be harmed by the second death.

## The Message to the Church in Pergamum

[12] "Write this letter to the angel of the church in Pergamum. This is the message from the one with the sharp two-edged sword:

[13] "I know that you live in the city where Satan has his throne, yet you have remained loyal to me. You refused to deny me even when Antipas, my faithful witness, was martyred among you there in Satan's city.

[14] "But I have a few complaints against you. You tolerate some among you whose teaching is like that of Balaam, who showed Balak how to trip up the people of Israel. He taught them to sin by eating food offered to idols and by committing sexual sin. [15] In a similar way, you have some Nicolaitans among you who follow the same teaching. [16] Repent of your sin, or I will come to you suddenly and fight against them with the sword of my mouth.

[17] "Anyone with ears to hear must listen to the Spirit and understand what he is saying to the churches. To everyone who is victorious I will give some of the manna that has been hidden away in heaven. And I will give to each one a white stone, and on the stone will be engraved a new name that no one understands except the one who receives it.

## The Message to the Church in Thyatira

[18] "Write this letter to the angel of the church in Thyatira. This is the message from the Son of God, whose eyes are like flames of fire, whose feet are like polished bronze:

[19] "I know all the things you do. I have seen your love, your faith, your service, and your patient endurance. And I can see your constant improvement in all these things.

[20] "But I have this complaint against you. You are permitting that woman—that Jezebel who calls herself a prophet—to lead my servants astray. She teaches them to commit sexual sin and to eat food offered to idols. [21] I gave her time to repent, but she does not want to turn away from her immorality.

[22] "Therefore, I will throw her on a bed of suffering, and those who commit adultery with her will suffer greatly unless they repent and turn away from her evil deeds. [23] I will strike her children dead. Then all the churches will know that I am the one who searches out the thoughts and intentions of every person. And I will give to each of you whatever you deserve.

[24] "But I also have a message for the rest of you in Thyatira who have not followed this false teaching ('deeper truths,' as they call them—depths of Satan, actually). I will ask nothing more of you [25] except that you hold tightly to what you have until I come. [26] To all who are victorious, who obey me to the very end,

To them I will give authority over all the nations.
[27] They will rule the nations with an iron rod
  and smash them like clay pots.

[28] They will have the same authority I received from my Father, and I will also give them the morning star!

[29] "Anyone with ears to hear must listen to the Spirit and understand what he is saying to the churches.

## REVELATION 3

### The Message to the Church in Sardis

**3** "Write this letter to the angel of the church in Sardis. This is the message from the one who has the sevenfold Spirit of God and the seven stars:

"I know all the things you do, and that you have a reputation for being alive—but you are dead. [2] Wake up! Strengthen what little remains, for even what is left is almost dead. I find that your actions do not meet the requirements of my God. [3] Go back to what you heard and believed at first; hold to it firmly. Repent and turn to me again. If you don't wake up, I will come to you suddenly, as unexpected as a thief.

[4] "Yet there are some in the church in Sardis who have not soiled their clothes with evil. They will walk with me in white, for they are worthy. [5] All who are victorious will be clothed in white. I will never erase their names from the Book of Life, but I will announce before my Father and his angels that they are mine.

[6] "Anyone with ears to hear must listen to the Spirit and understand what he is saying to the churches.

### The Message to the Church in Philadelphia

[7] "Write this letter to the angel of the church in Philadelphia.

This is the message from the one who is holy and true,
    the one who has the key of David.

What he opens, no one can close;

   and what he closes, no one can open:

[8] "I know all the things you do, and I have opened a door for you that no one can close. You have little strength, yet you obeyed my word and did not deny me. [9] Look, I will force those who belong to Satan's synagogue—those liars who say they are Jews but are not—to come and bow down at your feet. They will acknowledge that you are the ones I love.

[10] "Because you have obeyed my command to persevere, I will protect you from the great time of testing that will come upon the whole world to test those who belong to this world. [11] I am coming soon. Hold on to what you have, so that no one will take away your crown. [12] All who are victorious will become pillars in the Temple of my God, and they will never have to leave it. And I will write on them the name of my God, and they will be citizens in the city of my God—the new Jerusalem that comes down from heaven from my God. And I will also write on them my new name.

[13] "Anyone with ears to hear must listen to the Spirit and understand what he is saying to the churches.

### The Message to the Church in Laodicea

[14] "Write this letter to the angel of the church in Laodicea. This is the message from the one who is the Amen—the faithful and true witness, the beginning of God's new creation:

[15] "I know all the things you do, that you are neither hot nor cold. I wish that you were one or the other! [16] But since you are like lukewarm water, neither hot nor cold, I will spit you out of

my mouth! [17] You say, 'I am rich. I have everything I want. I don't need a thing!' And you don't realize that you are wretched and miserable and poor and blind and naked. [18] So I advise you to buy gold from me—gold that has been purified by fire. Then you will be rich. Also buy white garments from me so you will not be shamed by your nakedness, and ointment for your eyes so you will be able to see. [19] I correct and discipline everyone I love. So be diligent and turn from your indifference.

[20] "Look! I stand at the door and knock. If you hear my voice and open the door, I will come in, and we will share a meal together as friends. [21] Those who are victorious will sit with me on my throne, just as I was victorious and sat with my Father on his throne.

[22] "Anyone with ears to hear must listen to the Spirit and understand what he is saying to the churches."

# APPENDIX 2 - Violent Islamic Verses

The aim of these verses is to show that the motivation exists within Islam to wage an unceasing war on the world until mankind has been subjugated.

**From the Quran**

"And fight them until there is no more Fitnah (disbelief and polytheism i.e. worshipping others beside Allah) and the religion will be for Allah alone [in the whole world]. But if they cease (worshipping others beside Allah), then certainly, Allah is All-Seer of what they do." (Quran 8:9) (Translation from the 'Noble Quran'.)

"Fight those who believe not in Allah nor the Last Day, nor hold that forbidden which hath been forbidden by Allah and His Messenger, nor acknowledge the religion of Truth, (even if they are) of the People of the Book, until they pay the Jizya with willing submission, and feel themselves subdued." (Quran 9:29) (NB Suras 9 & 5 are the last "revelations" that Muhammad handed down - thus abrogating what came before. This includes the oft-quoted "Let there be no compulsion in religion..." (verse 2:256)

"But when the forbidden months are past, then fight and slay the pagans wherever ye find them, and seize them, beleaguer them, and lie in wait for them in every strategem of war; but if they repent and establish regular prayers and practice regular charity, then open the way for them." (Quran 9:5) (Islam sanctions violence as a means of coercing religion)

*"And fight them until persecution is no more, and religion be only for Allah." (Quran 2:193)*

*"Are they seeking a religion other than Allah's, when every soul in the heavens and the earth has submitted to him, willingly or by compulsion?" (Quran 3:83) (Again, this verse shows that Islam does indeed believe in compulsion for religion)*

## From the Hadith (records of the words and deeds of Muhammad)

*"The Messenger of Allah said, 'I have been commanded to fight against people till they testify that there is no God but Allah, that Muhammad is the messenger of Allah, and they establish prayer and pay zakat." (Sahih Muslim 1:33)*

*"When you meet your enemies who are polytheists (Muslims include Christians in this term) invite them to three courses of action...Invite them to (accept Islam); if they respond to you, accept it from them and desist from fighting against them...If they refuse to accept Islam, demand from them the Jizya (subjugation tax). If they agree to pay, accept it from them and hold off your hands. If they refuse to pay the tax, seek Allah's help and fight them." (Sahih Muslim 19:4294)* Osama bin Laden summed this verse up when he said, *"Does Islam, or does it not, force people by the power of the sword to submit to its authority corporeally if not spiritually? Yes. There are only three choices in Islam...Either submit, live under the suzerainty of Islam, or die." (The al-Qaeda Reader p19-20)*

*"Allah's Apostle said, 'I have been ordered to fight the people till they say: 'None has the right to be worshipped but Allah. And if they say so, pray like our prayers, face our Qibla and slaughter as we slaughter, then their blood and property will be sacred to*

us and we will not interfere with them except legally and their reckoning will be with Allah." (Bukhari 8:387)

"While we were in the Mosque, the Prophet came out and said, 'Let us go to the Jews". We went out till we reached Bait-ul-Midras. He said to them, 'If you embrace Islam, you will be safe. You should know that the earth belongs to Allah and His Apostle, and I want to expel you from this land. So, if anyone amongst you owns some property, he is permitted to sell it, otherwise you should know that the earth belongs to Allah and His Apostle." (Bukhari 53:392)

"Allah's Apostle said: 'I have been ordered (by Allah) to fight against the people until they testify that none has the right to be worshiped but Allah and that Muhammad is Allah's Apostle, and offer the prayers perfectly and give the obligatory charity, so if they perform that, then they save their lives and property from me except for Islamic laws and then their reckoning will be done by Allah." (Bukhari 2:24)

"The Verse:- 'You (true Muslims) are the best of peoples ever raised up for mankind' means the best of peoples for the people, as you bring them with chains on their necks till they embrace Islam." (Bukhari 60:80)

"And fight with them till there is no more affliction (worshipping others along with Allah."(Bukhari 60:40)

"Testify that none has the right to be worshipped except Allah, or else I will chop off your neck!" (Bukhari 59:643)

"Then the apostle sent Khalid bin Walid...to the Banu al-Harinth and ordered him to invite them to Islam three days before he attacked them. If they accepted then he was to accept it from *them, and if they declined he was to fight them. So Khalid set out and came to them, and sent out riders in all directions inviting the people to Islam, saying 'If you accept Islam you will be safe.' So the men accepted Islam as they were invited. (Ibn Ishaq/Hisham 959) (The text goes on to say that Khalid taught the al-Harinth about Islam **after** their conversion. This proves that it was based on fear of slaughter rather than a free and intelligent decision.)*

*"Therefore all people of the world should be called to Islam. If anyone of them refuses to do so, or refuses to pay the Jizya, they should be fought till they are killed." (Ibn Kathir)*

# APPENDIX 3 - Middle East Countries In Prophecy

Many scholars maintain that end-time prophecy always centres around Middle Eastern countries and that Western nations are never considered. Here is a list of nations that are specifically mentioned in prophecy. First there is the name by which they were known in Biblical times, secondly there is the name by which they are known today (if different), and then the verses where the prophecies about these nations can be found.

| | |
|---|---|
| Babylon - Iraq | (Isaiah 13-14, Jeremiah 5-51) |
| Assyria - Northern Iraq | (Isaiah 14:25, 30:30-33, Zephaniah 2, Micah 5) |
| Edom - Jordan and Arabia | (Isaiah 21, Jeremiah 49, Ezekiel 35) |
| Moab - Jordan | (Isaiah 15, Jeremiah 49) |
| Ammon - Jordan | (Jeremiah 49) |
| Damascus - Syria | (Isaiah 17, Jeremiah 49, Amos 1, Zechariah 9) |
| Gaza / Philistines - Palestinians | (Isaiah 14:28-33, Jeremiah 47, Joel 3) |
| Egypt | (Isaiah 19, Jeremiah 46, Ezekiel 29-32) |
| Tyre - Lebanon | (Ezekiel 28, Joel 3) |

Magog, Meshech, Tubal, Togarmah and Gomer - Turkey
(Ezekiel 38)

Persia - Iran (+Pakistan, Afghanistan)
(Ezekiel 38)

Arabia - Saudi Arabia, United Arab Emirates
(Isaiah 21, Jeremiah 49)

Ethiopia - Sudan                    (Isaiah 18)

Libya                               (Ezekiel 38)

Elam - Iran                         (Jeremiah 49)

# NOTES & REFERENCES

## Chapter 1

1. http://www.spectator.co.uk/features/9041841/the-war-on-christians/
2. http://www.breakingchristiannews.com/articles/display_art.html?ID=11702
3. . (http://www.civitas.org.uk/pdf/Shortt_Christianophobia.pdf)
4. http://www.christianpost.com/news/christians-most-persecuted-religious-group-in-the-world-says-expert-74332/#CAUz9TZKyZYKOcZF.99
5. http://www.monomakhos.com/its-official-christians-most-persecuted-religion-in-the-world/
6. http://www.france24.com/en/20110107-france-sarkozy-christian-religious-cleansing-middle-east-christians-coptic-bombing-egypt
7. http://www.monomakhos.com/its-official-christians-most-persecuted-religion-in-the-world/
8. Story taken from Jesus Freaks by DC Talk & The Voice of the Martyrs
9. Pew Forum 2011

## Chapter 3

1. It has been noted that the white horse rider carries a bow with no arrows suggesting he will conquer peaceably. The word "bow" is also rooted in the same Greek word as "rainbow", which became known as a sign of peace in the Old Testament.

This has led some to suggest that false religion and spirituality will make gains in the world through the promise of peace. Perhaps even world peace. The foundation for this theory is tenuous and so I didn't include it in the main body of the text. However, it certainly seems to fit with the tactics of the New Age agenda and is worth mentioning.

2. http://www.historytoday.com/blog/2011/07/alarming-increase-wars

3. http://www.trusselltrust.org/stats

4. http://en.wikipedia.org/wiki/Food_bank#Post_2007_financial_crisis

5. http://www.emdat.be/natural-disasters-trends

6. http://www.spectator.co.uk/features/9041841/the-war-on-christians/

7. http://www.youtube.com/watch?v=YogjYLtR8yY

8. Hebrews 11:35

9. "Your Best Life Now" is the title of Joel Osteen's 2004 book. Joel Osteen is the pastor of Lakewood Church in Houston, TX - the largest church in the United States (as of 2013).

10. People sometimes assume that if the church is 'not appointed to wrath' that automatically must mean they're raptured. However, notice that the 144,000 are not 'appointed to wrath' either but that doesn't signify a rapture for them.

# Chapter 4

1. Michio Kaku interview with George Norry, Coast to Coast, November 24, 2012, http://www.amateurastronomers.net/youtube-interviews.html

2. New Living Translation Bible footnotes

3. Daniel 10:20-21

4. http://www.pewresearch.org/fact-tank/2013/06/07/worlds-muslim-population-more-widespread-than-you-might-think/
5. http://www.islamicweb.com/history/mahdi.htm.
6. http://www.thereligionofpeace.com/

# Chapter 6

1. Jacob is another name for Israel. *"Your name will no longer be Jacob," the man told him. "From now on you will be called Israel, because you have fought with God and with men and have won." (Genesis 32:28)*
2. The Coming Prince by Sir Robert Anderson

# Chapter 7

1. http://student.kfupm.edu.sa/s200427200/images/caliph_history_mod.jpg
2. http://www.islamicweb.com/history/mahdi.htm
3. The same thing happens when date-setters try to prophesy the second coming of Christ. The more people cry wolf and get it wrong, the more scope it gives people to mock Christianity and the more discredit it does to the truth that Jesus *is* coming back.
4. http://www.bobsguide.com/guide/news/2013/Sep/16/world-payments-report-2013-unveiled-at-sibos-shows-non-cash-payments-to-top-333bn.html
5. http://www.mirror.co.uk/news/uk-news/tesco-using-minority-report-style-face-2674367
6. http://www.youtube.com/watch?v=bhKLz1boyyY
7.

http://www.theguardian.com/technology/2010/jan/11/facebook-privacy

8. http://en.wikipedia.org/wiki/Messianism

9. Ayatullah Baqir al-Sadr and Ayatullah Muratda Mutahhari, *The Awaited Savior,* (Karachi, Islamic Seminary Publications), prologue, p. 1

10. Sideeque M.A. Veliankode, *Doomsday Portents and Prophecies* (Scarborough, Canada, 1999) p. 277

11. Al-Sadr and Mutahhari, prologue, pp. 4,5

12. Abdulrahman Kelani, *The Last Apocalypse, An Islamic Perspective*, (Fustat, 2003), pp. 34-35

13. Kabbani, p. 231

14. Abu Nu'aym and As-Suyuti, related by Thawban, as quoted by Izzat and Arif, p. 44

15. http://www.mahdaviat-conference.com/vsdc%7D7q87a-2k,8.-y5a2.html

16. Tirmidhi as quoted by Mohammed Ali Ibn Zubair Ali, *Signs of Qiyamah* (Islamic Book Service, New Delhi, 2004), p. 42  and Prof. M. Abdullah, *Islam, Jesus, Mehdi, Qadiyanis and Doomsday*, (Adam, New Delhi, 2004), p. 54

17. Izzat and Arif, p.40

18. Sahih Muslim Book 041, Number 6985

# Chapter 9

1. There seem to be similarities between this "Gog and Magog" war after the Millennium and that described in Ezekiel 38 and possibly Ezekiel 39. I haven't reached a firm conclusion on this connection but leave it in the notes here as a possibility for further exploration.

More information available online at:

thefuelproject.org

facebook.com/thefuelproject

youtube.com/thefuelproject

plus.google.com/+TheFuelProject

Made in the USA
San Bernardino, CA
22 March 2015